THE CHURCHILL COALITION
1940–1945

THE
CHURCHILL
COALITION
1940–1945

J M LEE

Birkbeck College, University of London

Archon Books
Hamden, Connecticut

First Published 1980 in England by
Batsford Academic and Educational Ltd
and in the USA as an Archon Book
an imprint of
The Shoe String Press Inc.
995 Sherman Avenue
Hamden, Connecticut 06514

© J. M. Lee 1980

ISBN 0–208–01880–8

Made and printed in Great Britain

Contents

Acknowledgments

This book is partly a by-product of two specialist monographs and partly a personal celebration of the 'forty years on' since 1940. I accepted the invitation to write for this series when I was just finishing a study of the Anderson Committee on the Machinery of Government, and also an examination of the Colonial Office during the Second World War. *Reviewing the Machinery of Government: 1942-1952* was published privately in 1977, and *The Colonial Office, War, and Development Policy* which I wrote with Martin Petter will appear in the Commonwealth Papers of the Athlone Press. In writing the following chapters, I have often felt like celebrating 'the generation in between'—too young for war service and too old to be convincing radicals in the 1960s. My fellow sixth-formers at the Henry Mellish School in Nottingham, now 'thirty years on' from taking Higher School Certificate, will appreciate what I mean. Our lives were then still dominated by the consequences of war. Some friends may think that I have never quite recovered from being taught at Oxford by tutors just out of MI5 and MI6!

It is a pleasure to record my thanks to all who helped me with the two monographs, especially Martin Petter and Roy Wolfe. I am grateful to Lynn Claydon, Audrey Coppard, Caroline Cotterell, Pat Culshaw, and Joane Whitmore who all helped at different stages with the typing. Anne Daltrop was an excellent occasional research assistant.

Rodney Barker, Martin Petter and Michael Foot were kind enough to read and comment on my first draft. I have done my best to benefit from their advice.

J. M. L.
August 1979

Author's preface

This book is designed to help the student of political history in an appreciation of the regime which governed Britain during the Second World War. The coalition of all three political parties — Conservative, Labour and Liberal — over which Winston Churchill presided suspended many of the normal rules of parliamentary government, and gave the Prime Minister unprecedented powers to direct the war effort. 'Forty years on' — to use the title of Harrow School song which Churchill liked to sing — the government he formed in May 1940 is still an interesting subject to examine. It was the first administration to consider itself responsible for the welfare of the whole population. Churchill's leadership had some of the heroic qualities of a Roman dictatorship.

I have deliberately not placed events in chronological order. To have done so would have allowed the course of the war itself to structure the contents of each chapter too strongly, and distracted attention from critical features in the country's political life. I have instead assumed that my readers either already have some knowledge of the principal battles or can easily get access to a standard text-book about them. The 'Suggestions for further Reading' (pp. 181-5 below) offer guidance to the beginner. All the notes to each section are together (pp. 177-8). The diagram of the central executive (pp. 98-9) gives an overall view of government to which the reader should regularly refer.

After an introduction and two chapters on the general characters of the coalition, each of the principal chapters deals with a different aspect of government policy — strategy, economy, social reform and diplomacy. Although in that order international affairs are not handled until the final section of the book, it should be stated at the outset that ministers and officials were always aware of the impact of events overseas on all they did. Each of the principal chapters is an essay on a different set of opportunities and anxieties. It covers the content of policy as well as the character of the discussion and the machinery of implementation. I have not found it easy to strike the right balance between these components within the compass of a short book. I may have given too much space to the institutional changes. But then the essence of this regime was its adaptation of traditional institutions.

I have not tried to include any studies of character, apart from a few comments on Churchill himself. Nor have I treated the subject as if it were the history of relationships between ministers. The book is a little short on anecdote and local colour, although I refer to both biographies and diaries in the suggestions for reading (pp. 181-5). I sometimes wish that it were possible to present fictional characters in the form of autobiography. Basil Seal in Evelyn Waugh's *Put Out More Flags* (1942) and Widmerpool—typically it never seems quite proper to refer to him by his Christian name—in Anthony Powell's *A Question of Upbringing* (1951), which began the series of 'A Dance to the Music of Time', would have been excellent narrators of the administrative history I wish to follow.

I have also deliberately avoided discussing the 'caretaker administration' which Churchill formed in May 1945 and the General Election of that year when the Labour Party won a land-slide victory. Another volume in this series, Roger Eatwell's *The 1945-1951 Labour Governments* (1979), covers these events. It seems to me important too to avoid letting a discussion of the coalition be dominated by the knowledge of Churchill's subsequent defeat. Nor have I tried to use the literature of political science on the theory of coalitions. The war-time coalition did not fit easily into any of the categories that had been devised.

I have instead tried to convey an impression of the experience of governing. The subject is of course dominated by the accounts of those who 'had a good war', including Churchill himself. Their enthusiasm lingers on. Huw Wheldon, for example, in 1976 on the twenty-fifth anniversary of the Festival of Britain said that its organizers had worked with amazing speed because they had all enjoyed what he called 'self-fulfilling responsibilities' during the war. 'What nearly everybody had done was to take enormously experienced *ad hoc* quick decisions.' Much of the available literature still follows the interests and purposes of those who fought. Is it not now time to try and get beneath the emphasis on success to see the mixture of sentiment and motivation which drove the principal characters?

The main idea in what follows is that the government was compelled to combine the excitement of ruling largely by ministerial instruction with the perplexity of a massive extension in public awareness of the political. Ministers and officials were caught in an uneasy conjunction of bureaucratic inventiveness and popular suspicion. On the one hand, they had to find ways of stretching the rules of accountability to their absolute limits; on the other, they had to guess what impressions they were making without the benefits of public debate and informed press comment. Government rested upon a much more diffuse network of contacts than peace-time discussions of the Constitution would have contemplated. Furthermore, arrangements which suited the national mood of resistance to Germany in 1940 had to be adjusted to the entry of the United States into the war, and the expansion of military commitments on a world-wide scale.

Introduction

Contemporaries always found it difficult to decide which features of political life could be attributed directly to the existence of a coalition government and which to the exigencies of total war itself. Churchill's accession to power came after the basic steps to set up government by emergency regulation had already been taken; the acceptance of Churchill's leadership by the three major parties was an addition to an existing electoral truce and to an acceptance of the principle that the House of Commons could meet in secret session whenever it wished. Coalition was a new dimension to the operations of an administrative system which had already experienced many changes; its impact was not easy to assess.

The Labour and Liberal parties agreed to enter a coalition partnership without laying down any awkward conditions as the price of co-operation with their Conservative colleagues. Perhaps even more important to the success of the union, their representatives entered the government without inflicting pain and despondency on the party rank and file. Although there were objections to the idea of coalition and many private qualifications about the character of the Prime Minister as a politician, support of the new government was overwhelming both inside and outside Parliament. A. J. P. Taylor has called this administration 'the only genuine national government' which the country has had! Many of its members could remember the internal dissensions sown in the Liberal and Labour parties by the Lloyd-George coalition during the First World War.

The 'professionals' in the public life—ministers, senior civil servants, the commanders of the armed forces—had plenty of opportunity to reflect upon the consequences of co-operation between the major political parties. As the regime developed its characters, they were led to speculate about its future and direction. Different groups saw different advantages and disadvantages. Some emphasized the value of a government which expressed national unity and then realized that some elements in the popular acclamation of Churchill were distinctly a reaction against politics and all politicians. In 1940 there was a flowering of political pamphleteering, often in an extravagant and Utopian style. Others stressed the apparent lessening of the antagonism between social classes, particularly after the evacuation of schoolchildren from the big cities to the countryside in order to remove them from the dangers of war attack. But they then had to explain why so many members of the middle classes seemed to fear social collapse. The existence of the coalition did not remove doubt or controversy.

The most common approach of the 'professionals' was to think in terms of an emergency modification in the conventions which normally regulated Cabinet responsibilities and parliamentary debate. Coalition meant greater flexibility for ministers in deciding whom to employ and greater freedom for civil servants in calling for information and advice. It made it possible to create circles of confidence which ignored party affiliation. The whole of government could in some sense operate both with looser boundaries as the public sector grew larger and with tighter security when official secrets involved questions of life and death. If what Maurice Cowling calls 'the office seeking intelligentsia'[2] who came to positions of influence in the wake of coalition had any common perception of their own potential, they saw their opportunities in an expanded executive which interested itself in all aspects of the economy. This interpretation contained an assumption that the opportunities created for imaginative administration placed a premium on competence. As with the command of forces in the field, the manipulation of central government required the confidence that comes with proven ability. John Mulgan, whose *Report on Experience* remains one of the best reflections on action in war literature, even propounded the doctrine that 'men are no longer prepared for the inefficient and incompetent to flourish, by birthright or because they have friends in committee'[3]

There was a broad agreement inside government that a coalition of parties could withstand the inevitable unpopularity of administrative controls such as food rationing, the conscription of labour, and the commandeering of property. If the professionals stood together when imposing restrictions on freedom, they avoided the consequences of popular displeasure falling on a single party which acted alone. One of the strongest arguments for continuing in coalition after the war was that administrative controls might still be necessary while the country gradually returned to peace-time production. Some members of the administration were also interested in retaining coalition in order to build up an optimum programme in social reform. There was sufficient agreement on the need to improve secondary education and to provide better social insurance for hopes to be raised that a coalition legislative programme could be constructed. Others stressed the value of retaining coalition in order to have a bipartisan approach to foreign affairs in the international negotiations on the rehabilitation of Europe. They thought that the country should avoid making major questions of world order into subjects of party dispute.

The surviving evidence of these speculations now provides many clues about the character of the Churchill coalition. In so far as the representatives of different political parties inside the government retained a desire to pursue party advantage, and looked therefore for opportunities to exploit or bargains to be struck, they acted against the background of two very dominant anxieties. First, there was much concern about the long-term effects of the short-term arrangements which gave the government full control over the nation's resources. It was often thought that complete mobilization would bring some kind of socialism, or at least a permanent extension of state interference in private property. Many feared that the 'warfare state' would lead to a permanent 'welfare State' — to use the terms coined in 1941 by Archbishop William Temple. It is not surprising that many younger members of the Conservative Party thought that they had to embrace a more progressive approach to social reform and to recognize that more social services meant more expert administrators. Second, there was an equal concern about the fortunes of war itself. The price of victory seemed almost certainly to be a loss in international influence and prestige, if only a temporary one. The extension of the war in 1941 after the German attack on Russia and the Japanese attack on the United States underlined the fact that alone Britain was unable to defend the Empire and Commonwealth. Whatever the final peace settlement, Britain was likely to forego many of its previous advantages as a trading nation. The intrusion of American interests into the telephone network of Cable & Wireless, the oil installations of the Royal Navy, and the overflying rights of British Overseas Airways Corporation were all symbolic of the prospect that there could be no return to pre-war conditions. Ministers and officials saw their intentions and actions in the context of these two concerns.

For Churchill himself, never a strong partisan of a particular political party, the coalition was part of his personal dialogue with the nation. His sense of destiny depended on a profound knowledge of European history; his speeches on the defence of freedom and democracy appealed to popular recollections of Britain's contributions to the establishment of parliamentary government. From the moment of his accession to office he took steps to acquire the appropriate documents for his own personal archives in the hope that he would one day be in a position to write the history of the events in which he had played a major part. His six-volume history of the Second World War published between 1948 and 1954 still influences the way in which these events are examined[4]. As the war was being waged, he was defining its phases and turning points. He always contended that the war was 'unnecessary', because it could have been avoided if Britain had made a sharper response to the challenge of Hitler's Germany in the 1930s. As J. H. Plumb has noted, his appeal as a war leader was that he could make use of a past which had already died[5]. The coalition for him remained 'the most capable government England has had or is likely to have'[6].

For the rest of his administration the coalition loosened the rules of parliamentary government and facilitated the inevitable expansion of executive control. The authorities for the duration of the war recruited into the public service a whole range of scientists, dons, barristers, journalists and businessmen who would not otherwise have been given the opportunity to apply their intelligence to the practical problems of government. The existence of coalition made it much easier for those who had been associated with pre-war political agitation to offer their services. Those who had already been given a job to do had no compunction in setting out to recruit their friends. Many others sought to sell themselves and their skills to the most appropriate agency. Apart from the obvious desire to get into the armed forces, many ambitions to enter war work were quickly fulfilled. 'Back room boys' in the government research stations found themselves in the forefront of strategic planning.

The character of the coalition was already apparent at its creation. Churchill came to power after a revolt of Conservative MPs who challenged the authority of his predecessor, Neville Chamberlain. These rebellious supporters of the National government created such a mood of resentment in the House of Commons that the Labour party was compelled to reconsider its position. The Labour and Liberal parties agreed to support Churchill as the principal candidate who could save the situation. Ironically, the crisis of confidence in the conduct of war which provoked the revolt was about the defence of Norway for which Churchill, as First Lord of the Admiralty in Chamberlain's Cabinet, was directly responsible.

The government which Churchill formed commanded a majority in the House of Commons even stronger than that of the 1931 National Government. Unlike other coalitions, it was not formed merely to create a parliamentary majority for an alliance of parties which together could defeat the opposition. Churchill always had a built-in majority for his administration in the predominance of the Conservative Party, even if his relations with that party were not at first secure. The Churchill coalition was created to involve all interests in the nation, regardless of the number of parliamentary seats which each party held.

There were at the beginning some ministers who were prepared to contemplate asking the Germans to negotiate for peace. In late October 1940 when Hitler was laying down his conditions to a defeated France, Halifax as Foreign Secretary was drafting the peace terms which Britain might consider. But the majority of the government agreed with Churchill's determination to fight. Harold Nicolson noted in his diary on 5 November 1940 that Churchill's 'grim words' gave confidence rather than despair: 'we all feel, thank God that we have a man like that!'

The consent of the House of Commons to Churchill's authority as Prime Minister—and by extension to the consent of the people—rested upon his attitude to Hitler. While he was out of office from 1929 to 1939 he had acquired a reputation among Conservatives for being erratic and unreliable, particularly on such issues as the reform of the Indian constitution and King Edward VIII's right to marry Mrs Simpson. In May 1940 he benefited from being to all intents and purposes without a party affiliation. He was known primarily for his rabid opposition to Chamberlain's policy of appeasement and his tireless campaign for a British rearmament that would contain the ambitions of Nazi Germany. He became certain that Britain could not avoid declaring war.

The great virtue of Churchill's revulsion of feeling against Hitler was its grounding in history. His judgement was not based primarily on moral loathing but on an instinctive appreciation of the threats which German ambitions had brought to the balance of power in Europe. He argued not against Nazi brutality in German domestic politics, but against the danger of German strategic predominance in international affairs. He was particularly well read in the European wars of the seventeenth and eighteenth centuries.

'The Great Coalition' as he liked to call his administration was to him more a companionship of arms than an alliance of political parties. Bargaining between different party interests seemed totally inappropriate to its success. When its days were numbered in 1945, Churchill wanted to strike a medal which he could award to those who had been in its service, and even after he had formed a 'caretaker ministry' from the Conservative Party alone while the campaign of the General Election was under way, he held a reception to which he invited all his former colleagues[2]. Although in 1943-4 there were a number of different plans in circulation for continuing the coalition, the parties never seriously considered seeking a joint mandate from the electorate at a General Election. Whatever fears had been entertained that Churchill might emulate Lloyd-George and distribute a 'coupon' of approval to parliamentary candidates who supported him, the nature of the government precluded any repetition of a coalition receiving a mandate as in 1918. Victory in 1945 removed the basis of consent to Churchill's leadership.

Chapter one
War management

The impact of the coalition on the workings of government was akin to realizing the difference between the authority relationships of a training exercise and the panic of the battlefield. The retreat of British armies from Dunkirk and the fall of France induced a strong sense of stubborn resistance among the population at large. Churchill's rhetoric and blatant defiance of German military strength helped to rally support for the deprivations of total war. What had been a certain reluctance to take and use power became a flourish of executive ascendency. Those in authority sensed they could forget the normal constraints. Churchill expected to see firmness and dispatch among his subordinates. What had been a certain grudging acceptance of government regulation became a wholehearted devotion to the necessities of national survival. The threat of invasion confirmed that this was a 'People's War'. Although the government had no formal mandate and no means of seeking approval, it could rely on popular consent.

The agreement between the major political parties throughout the country was sufficiently strong to release a stream of energy into the institutions of the State and of private industry. Following the Prime Minister's example, officials and managers buckled down to the tasks of war management. Churchill's methods of work — particularly his habit of day-time sleep followed by toil long into the night and his rambling meetings for consultation — were often extremely irritating to those in his immediate entourage. But he provided a clear drive and showed that he was not only head of the government but also master of the civil service and the armed forces. However frustrating were the inevitable delays in government contract procedures and the delivery of precious raw materials, the managers of the leading companies saw the necessity for improved war production. The professional associations of managers with interests in industrial efficiency received a tremendous boost to their membership[1]. The application of scientific techniques to industrial production came into vogue.

The managerial tasks of government had somehow to be related

to the traditional machinery of the administration and normal out-
lets for political expression. The objectives were fairly easy to
define. The administration had to give even greater priority to
weapons production without endangering the economy by
excessive inflation or provoking popular criticism by allowing
manufacturers to make excess profits. Equally important was the
provision of sufficiently skilled men to handle all the weapons that
could be produced. Britain was so short of supplies and so limited
in the manpower it could mobilize that its political problems were
primarily about organization. How could what was available be
used more economically? Political life was reduced largely to
questions of manipulation to which there were no straightforward
answers. The 'professionals' in public life were not accustomed to
dealing with the political consequences of a war technology
dominated by aerial bombardment and high explosives.

Organizational questions seemed more immediately important
than financial ones. It was obvious that the country did not have
sufficient resources to sustain a long war without help from overseas, either the Commonwealth or the United States. Cabinet
assumed in 1939 that the war would last at least three years.
Officials assumed that sacrifices of overseas capital investment
could not be avoided. The Chancellor of the Exchequer in the first
coalition budget of July 1940 said 'What I need is cash and cash out
of current income'. It was a symbol of the new regime that this
budget introduced for the first time 'Pay as you Earn' — employers
were required to deduct tax from salaries and wages before paying
their employees — as well as a series of different rates in purchase
tax in order to limit civilian consumption.

Churchill acknowledged the importance of organizational skills
in his control of official appointments and postings. Although his
own style of management was idiosyncratic, he consulted the
Cabinet Secretariat when getting the principal members of his team
into harness. Constant sources of advice throughout the war were
Edward Bridges, the Cabinet Secretary, and his two deputies in
charge of military and civil affairs respectively, Ismay and Brook.
Indeed, the war was a turning point in the systematization of the
structure of the 'centre of the machine' as they called it. These
three did much to design the interlocking committee system which
divided the work of this War Cabinet[3] (see pp. 98-9). Churchill
adopted the device of having an 'inner circle' of senior ministers as
a War Cabinet which had already been used by Neville
Chamberlain. His choice of ministers was a gamble in finding the
most appropriate balance of skills between departmental responsibilities and inter-departmental co-ordination. While the coalition

lasted, the value of a minister lay less in his parliamentary standing than in his ability to hold together the committees placed in his charge.

Churchill also took care to make sure that the United States, although technically not a belligerent until December 1941, was nevertheless as fully committed to financing the war as President Roosevelt's inclinations would allow. A great deal of the negotiations between the two leaders was to tide over the period until the United States Congress could be persuaded to authorize the appropriate aid. The lend-lease arrangements which came into force in 1941 emphasized even more strongly the primary importance of organizational questions. Payment for war material could be postponed until after war.

The House of Commons was itself given a more bureaucratic role in that many of its 615 members wanted to take up places in the armed forces or the enlarged public sector, despite the rules which normally disqualify MPs from taking 'offices of profit' under the Crown. The existence of the coalition meant that the government front bench of ministers was no longer faced with an organized alternative administration. The most obvious division of the House was between those who held office and those who did not. The former category was enlarged when the government waived some of the rules of incompatibility which would have obliged MPs to resign their seats if they undertook official jobs.

During the first two years of coalition government those holding office quickly overtook in sheer daring and inventiveness the older generation on whom the initial burden of framing the procedures of mobilization had fallen. By 1942, in a total working population of 22 million, over 4 million were in the armed forces and their auxiliaries, over 3½ million in the manufacture of weapons and equipment, and 1½ million in public service positions. The first moves in 1939 were taken from the 'war books'—instructions on what to do if war was declared—which embodied the accumulated experience of the Committee of Imperial Defence. Officials who had learnt the difficulties of organizing war production in the Ministry of Munitions or the Ministry of Shipping in 1916-19 were recalled for service. But as the war progressed and as the presence of the coalition made itself felt, the characteristic problems arising from the technologies of total war were identified and new administrative devices conceived. As a general rule the First World War principle of starting with voluntary regulation was abandoned. National systems of allocation were used from the beginning.

Work in war-time central government did not require simply great care in taking precautions to preserve the security of military planning; it also demanded some ability in extracting information from unwilling colleagues or opposite numbers, without revealing the reason why. The organization of secret intelligence naturally had its own methods for providing 'cut offs' between its different circuits; the management of double agents required the most scrupulous taking of notes and keeping of records to preserve the consistency of the deceptions. But even outside such highly secret matters, officials were regularly involved in deceiving their own side or at least in avoiding a direct answer to a plain question. Ewen Montagu, a barrister in naval intelligence and after the war a leading magistrate and judge, has confessed to 'a lot of pretty skilful dissimulation': 'It was not only from my own work in deceiving the Germans that I learnt the fascination of the "criminal life" of fraud, false pretences and so on'[4]. To have no guile in the management of business was an insuperable handicap.

There were sharp contrasts between different rates of activity. Senior and trusted officials undertook an enormous workload; young recruits who matured quickly under the pressure of business were often perceptive enough to secure the patronage which brought a good posting. Fear of defeat and a certain unresolved guilt about the proximity of death for those in the field brought a manic drive to public administration. At one end of the scale, Sir Edward Bridges as Cabinet Secretary was regularly working a 16-hour day and taking only from Saturday lunch to Sunday lunch as his weekend. Officials in the Cabinet Secretariat slept in the cellars at the height of the German bombing of London. At the other end, there were long periods of enforced idleness, waiting for the operation that was never launched; or even an idiotic series of reposting and retraining for jobs which never materialized. The younger son of the former Prime Minister, Stanley Baldwin, seems to have been regularly and almost wantonly misposted, as if the officer corps could not handle an Etonian who wanted to earn a commission by working up from the ranks of the RAF[5]. Somewhere between these two extremes were the ineffective busybodies. Some units were designed to absorb the energies of the unreliable.

At levels where it mattered there was the minimum number of changes in personnel. The successful combinations built up before 1942 tended to stay together for the duration of the war. Each minister guarded his favourite officials; each director fought to avoid losing those with whom he had developed an expertise; individuals were less easily bribed with a promise of promotion if satisfaction came from position rather than rank. So many key organizations reflected the basis of trust which existed between the senior men, and even after the war these relationships influenced decisions about posting and promotion. The dedication to the task in hand had been so intense.

The authority of the administration was conferred upon those who could claim the support of the most prestigious elements in the government machine, whether they were eminent persons and men of influence or particularly successful units and committees which such people had created. Those who wished to press for a particular course of action had to be familiar with the reputations of the moment—who trusted whom, when and why. A respected chairman, such as Sir John Anderson as Lord President, might find the agenda of his committees taken up with items shifted from elsewhere. Central government became a vast concourse of contenders for 'courtly' authority—with 'the old man at the centre'—each putting forward his own set of solutions.

Whitehall as the centre of a complicated system of organizational politics was so absorbing in time and energy that those involved had little contact with the spontaneous political speculation of the 'front line' in the barrack room or air raid shelter. The 'professionals' in administration knew that they were in danger of losing touch with public opinion. The Ministry of Information devised a series of 'home intelligence' reports to provide a regular monitoring. The War Cabinet received regular reviews of the progress of war, and of events in the Empire and colonies.

Churchill himself always cultivated a sense of accountability for his actions to the House of Commons as the traditional 'inquest of the nation'. Even when it was clear that only a severe military defeat could dislodge him from office, he continued to show his respect of the situation. It symbolized his strong conviction that the war was just and provided a natural theatre in which he could demonstrate his sense of historic destiny.

But other ministers were less certain that the House could adequately reflect the changes which they sensed were taking place in the country at large. The House was still basically the group of members elected in 1935. The General Election required by statute in 1940 was regularly postponed year by year. The electoral truce agreed by the party whips in September 1939 applied only to by-elections. It was decided then that any vacancy which created the need for a by-election was to be filled by the party already in possession of the seat. The three party leaders commended the nominee of that party to the electorate of the constituency. But for the intervention of independents and of parties which did not respect the truce, the allocation of seats in the House of Commons would have remained frozen in pre-war proportions. Chamberlain's National Government also extended the electoral truce to local government by passing a law which enabled local authorities to fill vacancies by co-option.

It is not necessary to postulate a growing consensus between the parties in order to explain the Labour Party's position in the coalition. Its National Executive Committee did not originally want an electoral truce with Chamberlain's Conservatives[16]. But it was obliged to agree because of the physical obstacles to holding elections—air raids, the black-out of all lights, the evacuation of families and the difficulties of compiling an accurate electoral register. Even when Churchill's accession to power made the truce more acceptable, the policy commitments of the left wing of the Labour Party were not totally submerged in the experience of Labour Ministers within the government. Labour's acceptance of office did not rest on a unanimous decision to work within the existing institutions of the State, but on a feeling that the working class would be better served by going in rather than by staying out. Indeed, a major feature of the coalition was the determination of Labour leaders, doubting their ability to win the next General Election, to do what they could for working-class interests while the time was favourable. The Labour party through the accident of coalition gained a position which had never been envisaged in pre-war discussions on the possibility of a 'Popular Front'.

Nearly all the tensions inside the coalition sprang from the disputes of organizational politics themselves or from contrary interpretations of the effects of mobilization. Many feared that the systems of rationing and allocating raw materials would leave a permanent mark on political life. The very notion of 'fair shares' in austerity and the slogan of 'equality of sacrifice' seemed to suggest government might be permanently responsible for a more equitable distribution of national wealth. At least one war-time political organization, Common Wealth, advocated the expropriation of private property in the public interest. Some MPs thought that surveys taken of public opinion in 1941-2 showed how much more radical were the views of ordinary people than those of their elected representatives.

The impetus to the machinery of government provided by the coalition had been lost by the time the United States entered the war. The presence of Americans added a new dimension to the existing uncertainties. The influence of the American government had always been felt, but after the United States entered the war in December 1941, the very procedures of co-ordination had to be adapted. Both production and strategy became the subject of 'combined boards' or committees in Anglo-American co-operation. Indeed, by the end of 1942, the British administrative apparatus in

Washington was an important part of the national bureaucracy. The inter-Allied machinery which had been constructed by Britain and France in both 1917-18 and 1939-40 was completely surpassed by the size and scope of the Washington supply and production boards.

The coalition after 1942 was also increasingly exposed to pressure from American politicians and to appeals that each step in defining policy on major issues should be related to possible effects on American opinion. Not only did British and American officials have to educate each other in their respective conventions of government, but also British and American ministers had to compare and contrast the possible long-term effects of their respective methods in mobilization. The American authorities often set limits to British discussions on reconstruction without always having much sympathy for the practical difficulties which British industry had to face in returning to peace-time production. The imbalance between the 'mutual aid' arrangements which made Britain the debtor nation gradually began to influence the tone of Anglo-American co-operation. Churchill's own obsession with the greatness of the English-speaking peoples seemed to cloud his perception of the future of the alliance.

The major difference between the first and the second half of the coalition's existence was embodied in a shift of emphasis between the two major areas of concern in war management. The first half was dominated by the major macroeconomic choice of allocating resources between civilian and military users. How much could civilian consumption be cut to make available the necessary material for the armed forces? There were many awkward gambles taken in answering this question. Donald MacDougall has recalled how the figure proposed for cutting military shipping space in order to safeguard the level of civilian food imports in 1942 was not rounded up in committee as expected, so that the stock of imported food materials nearly dropped to danger level? Those involved in calculating the figures were extremely conscious of the tactics involved in getting committees to reach agreement. It was always necessary to combine science with guile.

The second half of the coalition's life was dominated by the geopolitical question of balancing British interests in Europe with those in the Far East. The British General Staff was never in a position to marshal sufficient forces for both a European campaign and a defence of the Empire routes over the Atlantic and Pacific. It was compelled by Hitler's actions to concentrate on Europe, and particularly on barring any German advance through South-East Europe which would threaten the British position in the Eastern

Mediterranean. British power in the Middle East and whatever alliances Britain could maintain with Yugoslavia, Greece and Turkey were the lynch-pin of its opening strategy in 1939-41. The Eastern Mediterranean covered both the route to the Far East and the main routes to oil and other raw materials; the western desert in Egypt and Libya was the most natural ground on which to take a stand as soon as France had fallen. But any concentration at this point left the defences against Japan in the Far East very exposed.

The United States was never placed in the comparable dilemmas of choice between different theatres of war. Its massive resources could be much more readily deployed. The trouble for Britain was that the predominance of the United States seemed to leave so many issues of postwar reconstruction unresolved. A whole range of what appeared to be technical questions in British policy, such as the re-allocation of war production factory space or the drafting of rules to limit industrial mergers, had an international aspect. Decisions often had to await the discussions of the American Congress.

The main ingredient of war management to survive the shift of concern in war management was the recognition that applied science, including economics and other social sciences, had validity in government service. The coalition's work permanently increased the status of what Lord Zuckerman has called 'disciplined observation' over *a priori* reasoning. The greatest long-term contribution of mobilization planning to future governments was the accumulated experience of economists, mathematicians and scientists in the presentation of policy choices.

Chapter two
Cabinet, Parliament and people

The whole population had anticipated the sacrifices of war mobilization before the Conservatives in the House of Commons failed to give Neville Chamberlain their full support. The political effects of a massive expansion of the system of administration were already being discussed before Winston Churchill came to power; and aspirations that war would compel the advancement of social reform were regularly voiced before the Labour Party joined the government. In the language of the times the endurance of conscription, rationing and evacuation were 'the birth-pangs of post-war England in the making'. There was a sudden flowering of literature on the opportunities of war, and many books and pamphlets were deliberately intended to disturb 'the governing classes'.

What the coup against Chamberlain achieved was to change the formal basis of popular consent to action already taken, without dividing the rank and file of the political parties in the country. The commitment to war itself had the backing of the overwhelming majority of MPs. The Independent Labour Party's motion in December 1940 in favour of finding a basis of peace was massively defeated in the House of Commons by 341 votes to 4. By-elections showed that the Fascist and Communist Party opposition to the war attracted few popular votes. The Gallup polls conducted on rationing to measure the impact of administrative regulation provided evidence that the population was generally willing to accept deprivation. What was missing in the extremely cold winter of 1939-40 was a sense of harmony between Cabinet, Parliament, and people. The division between 'us' and 'them' was exemplified in a propaganda poster at the outbreak of war which proclaimed: 'Your courage, your cheerfulness, your resolution will bring us victory'—us, *not* you! Back-bench Conservative MPs saw the incongruity of the government which they supported switching from a policy of appeasement to an application of defence regulations, and felt particularly sensitive to the charge that only business and capitalist interests were being incorporated into the apparatus of administrative control which required so many panels and advisory committees. The revolt of Conservative MPs against their own government was as much a response to the demands of their own political integrity in the national crisis as an attack on specific acts of incompetence.

The informal basis of popular consent had already shifted away from the traditional basis of party and Parliament towards the strange mixture of arbitrary dictation and voluntary effort to which the whole population was ready to accept. The 'governing classes' had reason to be disturbed by the literature directed against them. The war for civilians had opened not with a direct experience of battle but with the introduction of regulations based on the administration's experience of the previous war, rules made more imperative by contingency plans to disperse the population most vulnerable to bombing from the air as soon as war was declared. Government departments put into operation the instructions contained in the 'War books' prepared for the Committee of Imperial Defence, and the Ministry of Health went ahead with its instructions to evacuate schoolchildren from the big cities. (Even before war was formally declared, Neville Chamberlain had authorized the evacuation of schoolchildren). Unlike 1914-15, 1939-40 witnessed a massive civilian upheaval which compelled town and country to mix and social classes to observe each other's habits. The movement of three million people from congested industrial towns to the rural areas, and then their drift back home when the anticipated aerial bombardment did not begin, was an important political event which the 'governing classes' could not ignore. Furthermore, although the major item on the agenda, this evacuation was only part of an extremely complex set of co-operative enterprises which brought together central government, local authorities and voluntary agencies, such as the Red Cross or the Women's Institute. Consent to government action was tied closely to this involvement.

There was enthusiasm for postwar reconstruction from the very beginning of hostilities, and long before a coalition uniting the major political parties was conceived. The ideas, the drive, and the determination sprang from the preparations which had preceded the declaration of war, particularly after the Munich crisis of September 1938 when part of Czechoslovakia (the Sudetenland) was annexed by Germany. Britain began to prepare for war in earnest after the other parts, Bohemia and Moravia, had been occupied by Hitler's forces in March 1939, Slovakia having already broken away and declared herself pro-Axis. Knowing full well that it was virtually impossible to catch up with Germany in

technological investment for war—the lead time in the development of weapons seemed likely to be outpaced by the speed of
diplomatic failure in negotiation—the more perceptive and
enterprising civil servants and potential officers had devoted
themselves to the only available course of action, intelligent
preparation for imminent danger. Just as a sailing enthusiast could
volunteer for the Royal Naval Supplementary Reserve in the hope
of accelerated promotion for service at sea, the official with a spirit
for adventure had the opportunity of working for a 'shadow
organization'. In the eighteen months before war broke out, there
were not only 'shadow ministries' waiting to be revealed, but also
'shadow factories' and 'shadow firms'. Even the new organizations
prompted by the need to counteract Nazi propaganda, such as the
British Council and the European Services of the BBC, had 'shadow
purposes'. War did not at least come suddenly; it had already been
well anticipated in the blurred penumbra between officially recognized planning and the voluntary efforts of the patriotic.

The appointment of Winston Churchill as Prime Minister
provided both an appropriate focus for popular consent and a
source of patronage for technical invention. The new Prime
Minister was accorded unparalleled approval. Public opinion
polls—themselves an indication of the changing political climate—
recorded his score. By August 1940 eighty-eight per cent of the
sample in a Gallup poll approved of his leadership. With the
publication in July 1940 of *Guilty Men,* an attack by three
journalists on the colleagues of Chamberlain, Churchill was in a
strong position to reconstruct his ministerial team.

Even before war broke out, Churchill had placed himself on
important lines of communication concerning technical invention
and the preparations for a full-scale offensive. Some regarded him
as a kind of 'minister without portfolio' outside the Cabinet and
government but with inside information fed to him by discontented
scientists, soldiers and officials. When the Labour and Liberal
parties declined an invitation to join the National Government at
the outbreak of war, Chamberlain broadened his administration by
admitting two principal opponents of his appeasement policy in
the Conservative party, Churchill and Eden, in spite of the distrust
which they had both previously aroused. As First Lord of the
Admiralty, Churchill was able to indulge his patronage of technical
innovation and improved intelligence. His private office in
Admiralty House became a power-house of ideas which became
more influential as he improved his position in leading strategic
discussions, a role eventually recognized formally by Chamberlain
who made him chairman of the military co-ordinating committee.

Churchill's contempt for the 'professional' who protected an out-of-date expertise, or failed to relate his strategic knowledge to major political changes, struck just the right note of daring in the minds of those who hoped that social and political changes would follow the engines of war.

But, equally important, the appointment of Churchill as Prime Minister allowed the political parties to come to terms with the turbulent conditions of civilian mobilization which at the level of town and parish had upset the local structure of power. Lloyd-George remarked 'He will not smash the Tory Party to serve the country, as I smashed the Liberal Party.' The coup against Chamberlain in the House of Commons carried weight partly because of a general unease among 'the governing classes' that traditional bases of party support were being undermined in the welter of activity required for civil defence. The very basis of central-local relations was challenged by the appointment of regional commissioners, representatives of central government who were each charged with supervising the local councils in their areas and whose authority was supreme if the country were invaded.

The price of a successful coup in the House of Commons to bring a coalition into being was paradoxically the displacement of Parliament from the centre of the Constitution. The rhetoric of politics was centred upon Churchill's broadcast addresses to the nation. The edited and censored newspapers and other broadcasts came under the supervision of the Ministry of Information which after July 1941 was under the direction of Brendan Bracken, one of Churchill's closest associates. The BBC was the nation's heart. The practice of politics became in large measure a matter of individual and group survival in the apparatus of an all-embracing war machine. The aspects of mobilization from which the 'governing classes' had most to fear were the opportunities for political education which were presented not only by the barrack room and mess but also by the air raid precautions hut, the firewatchers' look-out, the meals kitchen or just the queue for rations. The strange alliances of adversity produced both a 'black market' for goods which were officially rationed and a 'street party spirit' in neighbourliness. In a moment of malicious frustration when Churchill's position as Prime Minister seemed somewhat precarious, Harold Laski writing in the *New Statesman* on 26 September 1942, said that Parliament had become 'Mr Churchill's privy council, and the general public his unseen audience'. The coalition had by its very existence transformed the rules of government.

The shift of allegiance

The key to this transformation was the adherence of Labour MPs to a genuine all-party coalition—a gesture which they could not make while Neville Chamberlain led the government. Their allegiance to a new regime had the approval of the party's executive which was holding its annual conference at Bournemouth at the time of the crisis. The Labour Party's executive meeting on 10 May 1940 declined to serve under Chamberlain but agreed to take 'its full and equal share as a full partner in a new government under a new Prime Minister who would command the confidence of the nation'. It assumed that the party's rank and file would support the leadership. The commitment of the Labour Party was not to Churchill in a personal capacity but to the destruction of Chamberlain's National Government and all its works. The parliamentary coup staged by dissident Conservatives was the culmination of widespread discontent in which the Labour movement played a larger part than its strength in the House of Commons would have suggested.

The extent of the shift of allegiance represented by the crucial division on 8 May 1940 can be measured in terms of Chamberlain's support. At the outbreak of war he had 418 supporters in the House of Commons while the Labour Party had only 167. With Liberal support the highest vote for which the opposition could hope was something less than 200. On 8 May only 287 voted with the government and 200 against. The measure of Chamberlain's decline was in the 80 Conservative abstentions rather than in the 41 Conservative supporters who voted with the opposition. Labour was in no position to force its way into the government; it came in at the Prime Minister's request because of its strength outside Parliament.

Labour's behaviour in the crisis guaranteed a coalition, but not a Churchill leadership. It might well have supported a government under Lord Halifax with Churchill as Minister of Defence. The selection of Churchill in preference to Halifax, although it was against the wishes of many prominent Conservatives as well as the King himself, seems to have depended on the grass roots of the Conservative Party. The new regime brought the formal parliamentary basis for popular consent into line with feelings in the country precisely because it had the guarantee of Labour's consultations at Bournemouth and the assurances conveyed in the Conservative Party through Kingsley Wood. What happened in Parliament in no way upset the rank and file of the major parties in the country. Beaverbrook's aphorism is in that sense correct: 'Not the King or the politicians wanted Churchill, but the people'.

The story of the choice between Halifax and Churchill on 9-10 May has frequently been told. The precise course of events and their significance will probably never be fully understood—there is so much personal myth-making in reconstructing the drama. But it seems clear that Kingsley Wood did play an important part in swinging party opinion against Chamberlain and in giving Churchill the impression he had sufficient party backing in the country in spite of the mistrust which he still induced in the 'professionals'. Chamberlain remained leader of the Conservative party until ill health compelled his resignation in October 1940. At that date it was impossible to prevent Churchill's succession to the party leadership, however dubious his claims may have appeared.

Labour's crucial role in creating the coalition did not earn its leaders a disproportionate number of portfolios in the Cabinet. Churchill made his first disposition of senior posts in strict accordance with the balance of the parties in the House of Commons—15 Conservative ministers, 4 Labour, and 1 Liberal. The new Prime Minister did not make a dramatic break with the past. Throughout the war and the life of the coalition at different stages and with a number of reshuffles only 15 people served in the War Cabinet—the small inner group of ministers who supervised the war effort—and 9 of these had already seen service in Chamberlain's War Cabinet. Only 5 Labour leaders were chosen for War Cabinet status and only Clement Attlee, the party leader, served at that level without interruption. At the beginning of the coalition Labour held 16 ministerial posts to the Conservatives 52; by March 1942 it had 22 posts, and by the time the coalition broke up, 27. These figures do not include the post of Parliamentary Private Secretary. Between 15 and 20 Labour MPs joined the government in this capacity.

It was often said that the two leaders of the Labour Party, Attlee and Greenwood, were much less capable than Churchill had hoped in holding together a number of key committees. Greenwood, who had a 'drink problem', was eased out of major chairmanships in 1941, and dropped from the War Cabinet in February 1942. Attlee's position as Dominions Secretary after February 1942 did not carry much weight, and he did not succeed to the position of Lord President until September 1943, just before reconstruction business was shifted away from the Lord President's committee.

The most stable element in the Labour Party's link with the coalition was Ernest Bevin as Minister of Labour and National Service. Although he was not admitted immediately to the War Cabinet, and before being given that status, had to wait a few months until Churchill was in a stronger position, Bevin like Attlee enjoyed the distinction of unbroken ministerial service. But unlike Attlee he remained in the same post throughout the war. He filled the government's key role in the management of industrial relations, and was therefore the embodiment of the support which the trade union movement had always given to the Labour Party. Under his guidance the Ministry of Labour and National Service came to play an important part in economic planning through its control over the use of manpower. Bevin and 'the direction of labour' in an economic sense—sending workers to where they were needed (a necessity which he did not at first admit)—became synonymous with Bevin and the 'Labour movement' in a political sense—keeping open the opportunity to improve the lot of the working classes. Popular consent to government through participation in war production, which involved all the consultative groups of trades unions on the factory floor, was channelled into the apparatus which Bevin supervised. Dissent was most likely to be felt immediately in strikes or other forms of withholding labour. The coalition was extremely dependent for its sense of legitimacy on the management of industrial relations.

Churchill's appointment of Bevin, inspired by an appreciation of the political assets which would accrue from a successful association of Labour's accession to power and a more efficient system of war production, was a symbolic gesture against his parliamentary colleagues. Bevin, although he had twice been a Labour candidate, had never been elected to the House of Commons; he gained his position in the Labour movement as general secretary of the Transport and General Workers' Union. Churchill was deliberately introducing a trades union leader into supreme position of power in industrial relations without choosing one who had a knowledge of Parliament. The party leaders had to find a vacant Labour seat for Bevin. He became MP for Central Wandsworth in June 1940.

The Labour party leader who embodied another strand in the expression of popular consent was Herbert Morrison, the leader of the Labour Party on the London County Council, who was brought into the Cabinet in May 1940 as Minister of Supply and then moved in the October reshuffle to be Home Secretary. Morrison remained at the Home Office which had the principal responsibility for air-raid precautions and fire-fighting, throughout the first months of the German night bomber attacks on London. The London 'political boss' was London's own Minister. Like Bevin, Morrison was in the same post for the greater part of the war. He had the right mixture of experience in local government manipulation and

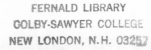

constituency party in-fighting to represent central government in the world of civil defence at the local level. The tension engendered by the mutual dislike of Bevin and Morrison was a price worth paying for the adherence of both.

The Labour Party's adherence to the coalition was more representative of the mood of the nation as a whole than its ministerial numbers implied, because it compelled some form-ulation of 'war aims' in both domestic and international affairs. If he had been leading a Conservative government, Churchill would not have been so easily restrained in the indulgence of his prejudices against social reform or of his racialist and reactionary views about world order and the future of the colonial peoples. He could and did divert the reforming energies of his ministerial colleagues into a number of subsidiary committees; he could and did take the view that while the war was being fought it would be foolish to occupy the time of senior ministers and officials with what he regarded as 'academic exercises' in planned reconstruction. But the concessions he made to reform inquiries and the very presence of reforming minds in positions of power set in train a series of discussions which he could not always control. He may have thought that he could regulate the energies going into domestic reconstruction by manipulating appointments; he may have assumed that the special relationship he had established with Roosevelt would counteract any lower-level negotiations on inter-national affairs. But the Labour Party's presence gave expression to precisely those interests in the country which had brought Chamberlain's government down, to the supporters of some attempt at social engineering.

The formulation of 'war aims' at home involved for the Labour Party a combination of planning for greater public ownership, particularly in the field of public utilities, and providing for a better informed and educated body of citizens. The Cabinet in October 1940 established a committee on war aims with Attlee in the chair, and created the Reconstruction Secretariat. Although the latter carried little weight in Whitehall, it provided a focus for all the many voluntary groups concerned about social policy. The winter of 1940-41 witnessed the creation of several movements for post-war social reform, and of inter-denominational co-operation between the churches. William Temple, the Archbishop of York, led a conference at Malvern in January 1941 to consider the Church of England's view of 'the fundamental facts which are directly relevant to the ordering of the new society'. The Church broke loose from some of its Tory Party associations, and later in the year the Labour Party began to sponsor working groups on individual reform questions. It was in this mood of enlightenment that the Army agreed to set up the Army Bureau of Current Affairs (ABCA) in August 1941, and to expand the services of the Army Educational Corps. Just as the Church of England had long been regarded as 'the Tory party at prayer', the ABCA in some people's eyes was too much like 'the Labour party in seminar'.

The idea of 'war aims' overseas did not come easily to the Labour Party which had many pacifist associations, and which in the 1930s had contained many who opposed preparations for war. Yet it was in many ways the party's reorientation in foreign affairs in 1939 that paved the way for its entry into the coalition. The party statement 'Labour and the War' issued in February 1940 was a clear commitment to the Allied cause. Although Labour ministers were not appointed to any of the key posts in foreign affairs—the Foreign Office, the Dominions Office, the Colonial Office, and the India Office—Hugh Dalton, one of Labour's junior ministers, took charge of the Ministry of Economic Warfare, with responsibility for the 'cloak and dagger' brigade of British agents behind enemy lines, the Special Operations Executive, which was both an overseas department and part of the war-waging system. Labour's presence in the coalition was a constant reminder of the party's traditional stance on the promotion of economic development in the Empire and on the furtherance of socialist governments in Europe. Indeed, it was Churchill's use of British troops in Greece in December 1944 against the Communist-dominated resistance movement which provided both a bone of contention within the Cabinet and a foretaste of future divisions in the Labour Party.

Churchill's personal style

Churchill's personal contributions to the coalition were the skills which ensured his own survival at the helm—rhetoric, the manipulation of contacts with other statesmen, and skill in exercising the sheer patronage enjoyed in powers of direct appointment. All these abilities tended to emphasize that party and Parliament were no longer the principal vehicles of political expression. Churchill's speeches were largely directed to the people; his private discussions with other statesmen were often not even reported to his own ministerial colleagues; and his personal appointments required special adjustments in the rules for holding public office. It is difficult in retrospect to imagine how frequently his colleagues asked themselves: how long can the old man go on? He remained both vigorous and resilient for one who in 1940 reached the age of sixty-six, a time at which others are content to retire.

Nearly all the assaults on his authority arose directly from the fortunes of war: when the Allies were fighting well, he was safe; when they suffered major setbacks, he was vulnerable. The period of the greatest uncertainty in both domestic and international affairs ran from December 1941 after the United States entered the war until November 1942 when American and British troops landed in North Africa. By the Summer of 1942 not only had the Japanese conquered the Far East but also the full thrust of German military power on the Eastern front had been set against Russia and German naval power had been deployed in the Atlantic.

Churchill made special provisions in case he was himself the victim of war or accident. In June 1942, as he was about to set out for the United States by air in a flying boat across the Atlantic, he suggested to the King that the latter should call upon Anthony Eden to form a government in the event of his own death[2]. Eden had in fact himself been speculating on his chances of gaining the succession, particularly during the period in 1942, when opposition to Churchill's management of the war was at its height. There seemed to be no other strong candidates on the Conservative side to match the bid for power which at one stage in Labour minds seemed to be within the grasp of Sir Stafford Cripps. It required a major military defeat to bring Churchill down. The loss of Singapore and the humiliation of seeing German battleships run through the English Channel in February 1942 seemed events which might change the balance of advantage.

Churchill's rhetoric and studied use of a classical prose style became the embodiment of popular consent to the war effort. All the mannerisms developed during a life-time in the craft of writing and in the business of government came to be valued for their qualities of national regeneration. Churchill's personal obsession with the political values of England, first given rein in the discussions which followed the Agadir Crisis in 1911, came to fruition thirty years later in his direct appeals for national sacrifice. No other member of the coalition could have commanded the same range of notes.

His contacts with other statesmen after a life-time in politics were in fact of less importance than the rather unusual and late addition to his armoury, the cultivation of his interests by President Roosevelt. The coincidence of Churchill's succession to the premiership and Roosevelt's decision to seek a third term as President brought a new significance to the correspondence on naval matters which Roosevelt had himself initiated with Churchill at the Admiralty after the outbreak of war. Even if the American President did not devote as much time as Churchill wished to

British problems until after he had survived his own re-election, the existence of the correspondence symbolized what the whole coalition knew, particularly after the fall of France in June 1940— that the undertaking of a long war in the last resort depended on American aid.

To many Americans Churchill *was* the government. But American aid was a product of Roosevelt's calculations of American interests rather than of Churchill's persuasive powers. Indeed, all the major steps had been taken to cement the alliance before the two men met in August 1941 on board a battleship in Placentia Bay to consider a joint declaration which became known as 'the Atlantic Charter'. Without any formal declaration of war Roosevelt had established the United States as the principal source of war production. Even before Britain declared war against Germany he had set in motion secret talks to secure American leases of British bases in the West Indies which were later to be traded publicly for the supply of destroyers to Britain. Before the fall of France and without consulting his own Departments of State and Defence he was encouraging a combination of British and French purchasing commissions to secure American aircraft. By October-November 1940, the ground had been well prepared for what Jean Monnet—the architect of Anglo-French co-operation then sent to Washington under British instructions—has called 'more intimate and open-handed methods of co-operation'. Roosevelt was able to move Congress from allowing supplies in November 1939 on 'a cash and carry basis' to accepting the principle of lend-lease in March 1941. The British purchasers changed from paying in cash and carrying in their own ships to simply taking delivery and leaving the bills to accumulate. Roosevelt's designation of the United States as 'the great arsenal of democracy' in a 'fireside chat' of December 1940 and his definition of the Four Freedoms in a speech of January 1941, expressed his total commitment to combating the Axis powers. When Harry Hopkins came to London in January 1941 as Roosevelt's personal emissary the financial basis of the Anglo-American alliance was close to being secured.

But Churchill's political survival also depended on the skilful disposition of the offices in his gift. He naturally concentrated on ministerial appointments and on commanders in the field. The upper echelons of the Civil Service were not as easy to manipulate, and he allowed its head and permanent secretary to the Treasury, Sir Horace Wilson, to continue in office until his retirement in July 1942, in spite of the fact that Neville Chamberlain had made that official into a special adviser. But on arrival in No. 10 Downing Street Churchill had removed Wilson from his room in that building. Churchill also turned down Wilson's recommendation of Sir Arthur Street to be the next Head of the Civil Service, and instead appointed Sir Richard Hopkins whom he had known in the Treasury when he was Chancellor of the Exchequer in 1924. Churchill exploited the situation which the involvement of senior officials in Chamberlain's appeasement had created in the public service. The Treasury lay under a cloud of culpability for the delays in rearmament, and the routine procedures of traditional civil service practice were out of tune with popular expectations for rapid strides in war production efforts. The Select Committee on National Expenditure's report on the Civil Service in November 1942 was in much greater demand than the normal run of parliamentary publications. The civil service trades unions looked for improvements in pay, conditions, and above all morale. With the addition of many temporary civil servants in central government, the time was ripe for many experiments in special teams and advisory units—almost 'private armies'—in which Churchill delighted.

His ministerial appointments in the War Cabinet itself were designed primarily to keep a party balance and to hold together the principal co-ordinating posts other than his own position as Minister of Defence. Throughout the greater part of the war Churchill and Eden were balanced against Attlee and Bevin as the principal representatives of the two major parties, while Anderson and Lyttelton brought in expertise in home affairs and production respectively. Morrison came into the War Cabinet after Cripps was moved to the Ministry of Aircraft Production.

During the course of the war forty-eight different people held posts of Cabinet rank outside the war Cabinet itself. Only one died in office—Lord Lloyd, the Colonial Secretary, in February 1941—all the rest were vulnerable to being moved or dismissed by the Prime Minister. The body of ministers left largely undisturbed were the service ministers and the law officers. Churchill in making himself Minister of Defence required secretaries of state in the service ministries who would work within the framework he created. The two senior members of the previous administration who were not included in the coalition government, Oliver Stanley and Sir Samuel Hoare, knew only too well what a difficult colleague Churchill had been at the Admiralty during the Norwegian campaign, because they had been at the War Office and Air Ministry respectively. A. V. Alexander (Labour) remained First Lord of the Admiralty for the life of the coalition, as did Sir Archibald Sinclair (Liberal) as Secretary of State for Air. It was indicative of Churchill's determination to keep a close personal control over the service ministries that he decided to make the permanent secretary of the War Office into the Secretary of State when he came to the conclusion that the military setbacks in North Africa compelled him to dispense with the services of David Margesson in February 1942. P. J. Grigg, the permanent secretary, stepped immediately into his own minister's shoes.

The Lord Chancellor's office and the law officers were left largely untouched in Cabinet reshuffles. Simon, who had been at the Exchequer under Chamberlain, remained Lord Chancellor throughout the war. Similarly, Somervell who had been appointed Attorney General in 1936 was allowed to remain in that office. Jowitt, the Solicitor General, was moved into reconstruction work in March 1942 and replaced by Maxwell Fyfe.

Other ministers gave steady service undisturbed; some indeed were able to establish fairly impregnable departmental positions — such as R. S. Hudson as Minister of Agriculture and Thomas Johnston as Secretary of State for Scotland. L. S. Amery at the India Office, at a time when the Government of India was directly concerned with constitutional progress in the sub-continent, had less personal power. Other long-serving ministers were Lord Leathers at War Transport, Brendan Bracken at Information, and R. A. Butler at Education.

In fact, only five junior ministers had three or more moves between different offices, and only nine were dropped and not re-appointed[4]. These 'casualties' included Caldecote who was promoted Lord Chief Justice and Ramsbotham who was granted a peerage as Lord Soulbury. Churchill also asked two others to agree to stand down in order to do him the favour of taking up special duties — Malcolm MacDonald to go to Canada as high commissioner and Lord Moyne to go to Cairo as deputy minister of state in the Middle East. Duff Cooper who was asked to undertake a mission to the Far East in 1941 was allowed to keep a Cabinet rank by being made Chancellor of the Duchy of Lancaster. In October 1943 Churchill wanted to have that office at his disposal. He persuaded Cooper to accept the post of British representative with the Free French and ambassador designate in Paris after the liberation[5]. Each of the 'casualties' who had no such face-saving refuge — Cross, Hankey, Margesson, Brabazon, Reith, and Tryon — saw that there were sound Churchillian reasons for their dismissal.

Churchill's indulgence in more fanciful appointments and his interest in units for special purposes outside the normal run of departmental organization were often stimulated by his immediate confidants, such as Brendan Bracken and Professor Lindemann whom he ennobled as Lord Cherwell in 1941, or by fellow politicians with whom he had a love-hate relationship, such as Lord Beaverbrook. Some members of the government thought that the 'cigar and brandy' circle had too much influence over the Prime Minister.

The 'old man' paid little attention to the doctrine of accountability to Parliament. The price of Churchill's freedom of manoeuvre in making appointments was an erosion of parliamentary commitments. The establishment of the coalition reduced parliamentary business. There were fewer sittings for the House of Commons which proceeded throughout the war with shorter sessions and a three-day week—usually Tuesday to Thursday—about 120 days a session instead of the pre-war average of 155. The House of Lords was similarly reduced to a two- or three-day attendance. The number of Bills introduced per session was drastically cut—from a pre-war average of about 180 to a war-time average of 54. The absence of a legislative programme meant that no standing committees were required, and the dominance of the executive led to the removal of special allocations of parliamentary time for private members.

Churchill himself took the leadership of the House of Commons when he realized that Neville Chamberlain to whom he had offered the post would not have been happy in it. Chamberlain accepted the position of Lord President of the Council which he held for five months until illness compelled him to resign. In practice, the leadership of the House of Commons until February 1942 was devolved on Attlee as Churchill's deputy.

Churchill managed the House of Commons throughout the coalition with a joint whips' office—the Conservative and Labour Chief Whips working in harness. This body also supervised the electoral truce by arranging for the writs to be issued for a by-election whenever a vacancy occurred. Initially, David Margesson was both Chief Conservative Whip and Secretary of State for War. James Stuart who succeeded him as Whip in 1941 remained in that office throughout the coalition, as did his Labour counterpart, William Whiteley, who replaced Charles Edwards in 1942. There was a form of organized opposition from those Labour MPs who did not hold office. This group elected its own 'administrative committee' to provide an opposition front bench. Although Attlee was still technically chairman of the Parliamentary Labour Party, while he was in the coalition this committee elected its own acting chairman—Lees-Smith in 1940-1, Pethick-Lawrence in 1942 and then Greenwood after he had left the War Cabinet for the duration of the war.

The principal scrutiny of the executive was undertaken by the

Select Committee on National Expenditure established in 1939 under the chairmanship of Sir John Wardlaw-Milne. Like the electoral truce itself, this device was both a legacy from the Chamberlain government and a confirmation of a First World War precedent. Wardlaw-Milne had originally been taken into the confidence of the government and shown the strictly secret returns on public expenditure in 1939-40. He was however reprimanded by Churchill in June 1940 for leading the Select Committee outside its terms of reference, and as backbench MPs began to settle into the parliamentary routines of coalition, he came to provide as much a centre for the criticism of organization and administrative incompetence as for the examination of expenditure. The other more informal device for scrutinizing the executive, the 'Watching Committee', a combination of Conservatives from both the Lords and the Commons under the chairmanship of the fourth Marquess of Salisbury, which had made direct representations to Ministers in the first two years of war, became much less important during 1941.

Churchill deliberately encouraged MPs to accept appointments which in normal peace-time conditions would have been regarded as incompatible with parliamentary duties. When he wished to appoint Malcolm MacDonald to be British High Commissioner in Canada in succession to John Buchan, Lord Tweedsmuir, who died in 1940, Churchill introduced legislation which would permit him to issue certificates that could override the application of the normal rules of disqualification for MPs who accepted 'offices of profit'. MacDonald wished to retain his seat in the House while he was away. When the legislation was introduced in February 1941, about 200 MPs were already engaged in some form of government service, and another 116 were in the armed forces. Churchill's insistence on acquiring the power to issue certificates which waived the normal rules, and on making the issue a matter of confidence in his government, revealed the vulnerability of Parliament to the Prime Minister's arbitrary demands. Some MPs feared that all members would become 'place men' in the service of the executive. The House decided to appoint a Select Committee under Sir Dennis Herbert to examine the problems raised, but its report was too complicated for the government to consider its recommendations.

Parliament was not therefore a forum for attacks on the idea of coalition itself, but only the place in which any direct challenge to Churchill's personal position had to be staged. The weakness of the Commons as a debating chamber and the special character of parliamentary management under the coalition meant that

Churchill normally lost reputation and standing whenever opinion in the country swung against him. If Chamberlain was removed from office by a parliamentary coup reflecting the feelings of the party rank and file, Churchill could only have been compelled to resign by an 'administration' coup which sought to find a scapegoat for disaster. Churchill's position was most obviously threatened by losses in battle which frightened the nation, and by reversals in the State's standing in international affairs which endangered its future. The major crises of his administration stemmed directly from external assaults.

The principal parliamentary attacks on Churchill in February and in June/July 1942 were ostensibly about the organization of war production, with its requirements in economic and physical planning, and about the organization of the high command, with its relationships between civilians and military. But they were just as much a reflection of the political mood of the country as a withdrawal of personal support from Churchill. Cabinet Ministers from all parties remained loyal to the Prime Minister during the period of military defeat—the loss of the Far East to the Japanese and the retreat in the western desert—except Sir Stafford Cripps who seemed to provide the only rallying point for an alternative administration. Cripps had returned from being British Ambassador in Moscow, bathed in the glory of popular respect for Soviet resistance to the Germans and keen to gain support for an Allied landing in Europe—a Second Front—to divert German efforts against Russia. Churchill felt obliged to invited Cripps to join the War Cabinet as Lord Privy Seal, and then skilfully weakened Cripps's position by appointing him to the Leadership of the House of Commons, a post which exposed his shortcomings, and by sending him on a mission to India. Popular disillusionment with the management of the war on which Cripps's appeal depended did not carry sufficient weight in the House of Commons to deprive the coalition of its parliamentary support. Churchill survived, partly because Parliament did not at that time fully represent the feelings of the nation. MPs were not prepared to overthrow the established authority. Wardlaw-Milne's motion of censure in the House of Commons that 'this House[3]...has no confidence in the central direction of the War' in July 1942 was lost by 476 votes to 25, with some forty abstentions. The majority of MPs were not at the time aware of Allied plans for landing in North Africa, nor of the achievements of Auchinleck at the first battle of El Alamein in holding the enemy advance.

Cripps, who hesitated a number of times over the tactics and purpose of resigning from the Cabinet, agreed not to hand in his resignation as Lord Privy Seal until after the campaign in North Africa had begun. After the second battle of El Alamein (23 October-2 November) the scales were being tipped in Churchill's favour and after the landings in North Africa (8 November) he was able to deal with Cripps by shifting him to the Ministry of Aircraft Production and bringing Morrison into the War Cabinet. Churchill implied that Cripps had chosen the wrong issue on which to resign — the direction of war. He told Cripps on 2 October: 'You are an honest man. If you had been Lloyd-George, you would have resigned on the issue of a second front'[6].

Reconstruction and the chances of coalition

When the tide turned in the fortunes of war during 1943, politicians and officials braced themselves for the tasks of reconstruction, but with different degrees of enthusiasm and anxiety according to their interpretations of what the experience of war had done to the basis of popular consent to government. The prospect of victory revealed just how fragile the coalition had been, and how much popular aspirations had been affected by the large numbers of people who had direct experience of war organizations. The publication of the Beveridge Report — the report of the Committee on Social Insurance and Allied Services, a departmental inquiry of the Reconstruction Secretariat — on 1 December 1942 opened the season of political speculation, coming as it did immediately after the victories in the western desert.

The prospect of victory also drew attention to British losses in overseas investment. Ministers and officials, regardless of their different conceptions of social welfare, hesitated to open a public debate about the effects of war-time sacrifice on the nation's peace-time balance of payments. The future looked grim. How effectively could manufacturing industry sustain a level of exports after the war that would tide the country over the period of transition, until the traditional strength of the economy overseas — the 'invisible exports' of banking, insurance, and shipping — had been recovered? The price of victory was going to be acute overseas indebtedness. Britain's weakness consisted partly of losses to other members of the sterling area and partly of the massive imbalance in favour of the United States in the mutual aid arrangements. India, for example, had taken advantage of British payments to support troops in the sub-continent to run up large sterling balances as well as to insist on buying out British investments. The repatriation of British capital holdings in the United States was a condition of the lend-lease agreement. British aid to the United States cancelled only a small part of the 30,000 million dollars of American aid to Britain. Only Canada which was closely involved in lend-lease made Britain an outright gift.

The public face of the coalition was judged at the annual renewal of the order prolonging the life of the 1935 Parliament. The prolongation, a matter of routine while the battles were still unresolved, became the subject of controversy as soon as victory was in sight. In October 1942 the end of the war still seemed far away, but in October 1943 the prospect of peace seemed not too far distant, although the Allied invasion of Europe had still to be mounted and completed. The prolongation for 1943-4 was regarded as the last that could be made without a full consideration of the time-table of the 'transition' from war to peace. During the spring and summer of 1943 the concept of a 'two stage ending' was developed and elaborated—first the defeat of Germany and second the switch of resources to a full-scale assault on Japan. Planning for the transition was handicapped by uncertainty about 'stage two'—how long would the war continue in the Far East after peace in Europe?—and by the grim prospect of what amounted to a 'stage three'—the period of acute British dependence on American resources as the country made its industrial recovery.

During 1943 the Allies also began to hold meetings to determine the scope of the proposed United Nations Organization and the agencies which it would have at its command. The Foreign Office set up its own examination of the 'international problems of the transitional period'. It was particularly anxious to restrict the terms of reference of the proposed U.N. Relief and Rehabilitation Agency. Plans for the rehabilitation of Europe went hand in hand with those for its invasion.

The mood of Cabinet ministers changed in October 1943. What Dalton in his diary called 'the remarkably good and important Cabinet' on 21 October approved the directive which the Prime Minister then forwarded to all departments asking them to prepare plans for the 'transition' from war to peace. In the Cabinet Office at this stage the working party on employment policy began meeting almost daily in order to hammer out the basic assumptions of economic policy which were eventually published in the White Paper on employment in June 1944. The government machine during the nine months between October 1943 and June 1944 was geared to a high pitch not only for the invasion of Europe but also for the frenzied round of meetings on reconstruction planning. In November 1943 Churchill was finally prevailed upon by his colleagues to appoint a Minister of Reconstruction. He persuaded a reluctant Woolton to accept the new post, to the great relief of his Labour colleagues who feared that they might have Beaverbrook thrust upon them. Even more important from the point of view of the official world, he approved the transfer of Norman Brook, the deputy secretary (Civil Affairs) in the Cabinet Office, to be Woolton's permanent secretary. The subject of reconstruction was thus given the highest possible status—the old 'Reconstruction Secretariat' which had ambled along through the height of the battle was totally transformed.

The priorities judged most important in the eyes of the electorate at a General Election, whenever it came, were the issues of security of employment and availability of education. The question of providing government guarantees to maintain a high level of employment seems to have arisen directly from the private discussion by officials of Beveridge's proposals for social insurance. Beveridge himself picked up the message from his contacts with the official inquiry and instigated his own private investigation. During 1943-4 there was a degree of rivalry between officials in the Cabinet Office and Beveridge's own staff with both attempting to work out a declaration of intent. In November 1943 the Treasury issued instructions that no official assistance was to be given to Beveridge. The government's White Paper on employment published in June 1944 preceded Beveridge's *Full Employment in a Free Society* by five months, but it was much less far-reaching than what Beveridge proposed. The Education Bill embodied the most comprehensive piece of post-war social policy in the coalition's reconstruction plans. It was the product of very extensive consultations conducted by the Board of Education, particularly with Church leaders whose control over primary schools and interest in religious education gave them an important say in proposals which amounted to creating a secondary education system for all children. The initial plans were drawn up by officials who had been moved to Bournemouth in the anxious winter of 1940-41 immediately after the experience of evacuation; the government's White Paper did not appear until July 1943 and its Bill until December 1943. Churchill and Anderson in 1941 had advised Butler, the minister responsible, 'to work behind the scenes'.

The priorities in the eyes of the Civil Service managers of the government machine were relieving the pressure on the parliamentary time-table that was likely to be caused by reconstruction legislation, and attempting to achieve a comprehensible pattern for the boundaries and functions of central and local authorities that would bear the burden of implementing policy. Among senior ministers and officials the reforms of Parliament and the revision of the machinery of government assumed a new if fairly discreetly acknowledged importance. The first moves had been made in confidence without any publicity. In January 1943 Sir Cecil Carr, the editor of the Revised Statutes, was asked to survey the subject of parliamentary procedure from the point of view of the executive; in June 1943 Sir Claud Schuster, the permanent secretary of the Lord Chancellor's office, was asked to chair an official meeting which would devise a programme for dismantling defence legislation. But the local authority associations feared that any reforms agreed upon within the coalition would lead to the creation of regional authorities or at least to a great reduction in the powers of local councils. They mounted a much publicized campaign of agitation. The Ministry of Health's plans for a 'National Health Service' brought the issue of local government reform to a head before any positive moves had been made in framing reconstruction policy. The Prime Minister was persuaded to make a statement on 22 September 1943 that the coalition was pledged not to weaken local government any further. Plans therefore were laid on the assumption that the main principles of central-local relationships would be maintained. By the time a Minister of Reconstruction had been appointed the way was open for central government to set its policies in the framework of a revised approach to the process of legislation, and in particular to the future of the emergency laws and defence regulations.

It was characteristic of the strain imposed on the coalition by the demands of planning that reconstruction should have been considered at a number of different levels and within different circles of trust. The back-benchers in the House of Commons who had been excluded from so many war policy questions fought their way back into the limelight as the prospect of peace loomed larger. Towards the end of 1942 a group of Conservatives under Sir Herbert Williams formed themselves into an informal committee of 'Active Back-Benchers'; another group under Sir Cuthbert Headlam met regularly to consider proposals for constitutional reform. There was also a secret committee of Conservative MPs to consider the Beveridge Report. Some Labour back-benchers, such as Shinwell and Wilmot, were closely concerned with the activities of a committee set up by the party executive on 'social and economic transformation in Great Britain'. The Conservative and Labour Party conferences in the summer of 1943 resounded with the products of working party activity. To Churchill's annoyance, Morrison began to suggest openly that the Labour party should beware of the concept of 'transition'.

The government's annual motion to extend the Emergency Powers Act for another year, like the application to prolong the

Parliament, was a ritual which changed its meaning with the prospect of victory. But 1943 it had come to symobilize the executive's vulnerability to back-bench restlessness. MPs began to express themselves very forcibly against the flow of statutory rules and orders which the government laid on the table of the House under its exceptional war-time powers of delegated legislation. A body of opinion, led by the 'Active Back-Benchers', was gradually created in favour of appointing a special 'scrutinizing committee' which would then draw the attention of the whole House to these orders which merited a wider debate. The executive's special interest in finding parliamentary time for reconstruction legislation was in danger of being thwarted by parliamentary concerns about the absence of an adequate machinery to scrutinize the law. By May 1944 a motion to appoint a scrutiny committee collected 140 signatures among MPs, and in June 1944 the government came forward with its own proposals and set up the Select Committee on Statutory Rules and Orders. The coalition's control of the House prevented the setting up of a Select Committee on Procedure.

The leaders of the Conservative and Labour parties while together in government preferred to act in concert and in confidence where they could do so. At one level and in public they sponsored the Speaker's conference to consider the reform of the franchise and the redistribution of parliamentary seats. It was widely believed that the next General Election was going to be fought on an electoral register which equalized the parliamentary and local government conditions for the right to vote. Many hoped for the removal of such anomalies as the franchise of business premises and of university graduates. The Speaker of the House presided over a conference to discuss these questions between February and July 1944, and preparations for the new voters' lists to come into force in April 1945 were set in train. But it proved more difficult to get agreement on the franchise than on the redistribution of seats. The Redistribution of Seats Act passed in 1944 increased the size of the House of Commons from 615 to 640, and established a Boundary Commission to make regular adjustments in constituency boundaries according to population growth and distribution.

At another level and in the confidence of Cabinet committees the party leaders sponsored a private inquiry by officials into the practical possibility of facilitating the progress of legislation—how government might increase its control over parliamentary time. That inquiry which worked largely from January to June 1944 explored ways of devising procedures in the handling of rules and orders laid on the table of the House which compelled private members, rather than government Whips, to take the initiative if they wished to drum up support against a specific piece of legislation. The party leaders also sponsored inquiries into the future of the departments set up for war purposes, and into the central departments that would be needed to administer new social legislation. It seemed important to avoid wherever possible bringing forward legislation to create the machinery as well as to define the policy, if short cuts could be found by creating general powers. The idea of legislating to allow functions to be transferred between ministers by statutory order emerged from all these different inquiries. The great advantage to coalition ministers of confidential official committees was that the Parliamentary Counsel and the Officers of Parliament could be consulted as well as civil servants.

The lessons of the war economy in fact had their official and their popular versions. The political 'professionals', both ministers and civil servants, in the intimacy of coalition were together drawing rather different conclusions from those drawn by the rank and file of the major parties, for whom war had aroused new hopes and fears. The prospect of planning and control which exercised the minds of the 'professionals' in preparing for the transition from war to peace was likely to polarize opinion in the country. War organization was manifestly more attractive to the official mind than to public opinion. When the party organizations in the country which had been run down during the early part of the war began to consider in 1943 which issues would revivify their supporters, they found themselves drawn away from the middle ground. The Tory Reform group which wanted to press for social reform was less likely to have a specific party appeal than those groups which reacted strongly against the direction of industry, such as Aims of Industry, the National League for Freedom and the Society of Individualists. The Labour party was similarly finding that its more radical members who pressed for land nationalization had a strong party backing.

Perhaps the strongest influence on political debate was not the Labour party apparatus itself but the literary intellectual movement which had progressive leanings—the social realism associated with *Picture Post,* the Penguin Book specials, and documentary films. The Common Wealth Party under Sir Richard Acland which in 1942 brought together a number of reformist groups was the organizational expression of this national mood. Its approach was on lines laid down in some of J. B. Priestley's broadcasts, and its support came very much from suburban middle-class areas. Although it began to place its members in Parliament at by-elections, it never seems to have damaged Labour's position.

Common Wealth candidates took votes from Conservatives.

Because the making of the coalition had not damaged the structure of political party support in the country, with all its characteristic class associations and ideologies, there was no serious obstacle to the return of party government. Indeed, popular interest in politics tended to drive the leadership towards the break-up of coalition perhaps more quickly than leading politicians would have liked. The delay in overcoming the technical problems in mounting the election of a new Parliament—the preparation of a new electoral register and the provision of adequate postal voting for the armed services overseas—provided a long lead time in speculation and hesitant manoeuvre.

Being dominated by memories of the major precedent in a post-war return to elections—Lloyd-George's management of the 'coupon election' in 1918 at which Labour had refused to remain in coalition but had been defeated by the two major parties which did—the 'professionals' were mindful of the electoral advantage which Churchill himself might give to the Conservatives or to any combination with them which he cared to create. The Labour Party 'faithful' did not wish to get embroiled in any tactical calculations about joining a 'national government'. Harold Laski, as Chairman of the party, was deliberately choosing a sensitive spot when in May 1944 he accused Attlee of 'MacDonaldism'—the sin of consorting with the friends of capitalism. Attlee at that stage was quite clear in his mind about the need to hold the government together in the 'interim period'. In his reply to Laski on 1 May he said 'there is inevitably a compromise': the transition could not be based on either socialist or capitalist principles. Attlee accepted the need to compromise because 'the country had got to play a big part in shaping the post-war settlement'[8].

Calculations of the consequences of dismantling the coalition were made at many different levels of informed opinion. Churchill himself was in many people's eyes fairly remote from the world of gossip. As Chamberlain had been lulled by the shift in Kingsley Wood's loyalties, Churchill was in danger of seeing the future too much according to the vision of Beaverbrook, Bracken and Cherwell. Very few intimates shared his knowledge that the atomic bomb might change the shape of all strategic plans for the defeat of Japan and thus telescope the process of 'transition' itself. The second stage of the 'two stage' ending of the war depended entirely on the strategic means available. In Britain at any rate where public opinion had been educated to see the war much more in anti-German than in anti-Japanese terms, it was obviously going to be harder to maintain sufficient drive and cohesion for a war effort in the Pacific. The second stage even more than the first was an American operation. Opinion in the United States was more strongly focused on Japan than on Germany.

The dilemmas of those calculating the risks of changing the political regime of the government lay in the uncertainties of demobilization. How quickly and how many resources could be transferred from the war effort to preparing industry for the 'battle of exports' as soon as the war with Germany had been satisfactorily concluded? This was the major 'professional' question in planning. How far and how rapid would be the transfer of manpower from the armed services to well-paid civilian employment which was the 'popular' question of practical politics? As with the prospect of a General Election, the precedents which many thought should *not* be repeated were the arrangements made in 1918-19. A great deal of effort during 1944 was put into the planning of demobilization. Bevin and his department, the Ministry of Labour and National Service, gave the lead in linking demobilization plans with economic and employment policy. By the time Bevin announced in September 1944 what had been decided for the armed forces and the civil service it had become increasingly difficult to hold key individuals in their posts. The population mobilized in 1939-40 had by 1944 become extremely restless.

Ministers and officials in the coalition read the signs in Parliament and at by-elections. The House of Commons developed an increasingly partisan atmosphere after the winter of 1942-3, and particularly after public discussion of the Beveridge report. On 9 February 1943, 116 Conservatives voted against the Catering Wages Bill introduced into the House by Bevin as Minister of Labour. They saw the measure as the beginning of greater government intervention, an attempt to institutionalize emergency regulations on minimum wages and conditions of work, but their stand prompted members of their own party to nail their colours to the mast of social reform. The Tory Reform Group created in March 1943 was a direct consequence of this parliamentary division, and that group based its cause also on the Beveridge Report which had split the Labour party. After the debate in the Commons on that report on 16-18 February 1943, 97 Labour members including Greenwood himself voted against the government's lukewarm reception of the proposed reforms in social insurance. The 'professionals' began to see the dangers of being isolated from the rank and file.

From February 1943 onwards parliamentary candidates standing in by-elections on behalf of the coalition felt increasingly vulnerable to Independent Socialists or to the Common Wealth Party. The latter's candidate won the Eddisbury division from the Conservatives in April 1943 and, perhaps most damaging of all to Conservative reputations, an independent socialist in February 1944 deprived the Duke of Devonshire of the privilege of placing his son, Lord Hartington, in the House of Commons as member for West Derbyshire, a constituency which had been in the patronage of the family for many years. Those who interpreted the by-election results during the last year of the coalition had fairly unequivocal evidence of a trend towards the 'socialist' candidates. Between the Eddisbury election and the collapse of the coalition, four Conservatives supporting the government were defeated.

In March 1944 Transport House told the Labour party committees throughout the country to begin to rebuild their electoral organization, in spite of the confidence expressed by some Labour leaders in the future of the coalition. At a private conference of Labour 'influentials' held at Dartington Hall in the same month, all the speakers reported finding a general cynicism and bewilderment in the constituencies about the future of party politics. Sir Stafford Cripps, George Strauss and Michael Young led a discussion on Labour's chances in the next election. This kind of discussion was repeated very frequently over the course of the next year as the Allied armies pressed forward in Europe. By October all the major parties were equipped for another election. On 31 October Churchill committed himself to dissolving Parliament as soon as a victory over the Germans had been secured. The two-stage ending was to be divided not simply in strategic and resource terms but also by electoral results. Whoever led the country at the second stage would be committed to providing sufficient British resources for victory over Japan.

Several Labour leaders would have preferred to stay in office under a coalition at least until the war against Japan had been completed. They were caught by the coincidence that the Labour Party Conference at Blackpool had been arranged for May 1945, just a few days after what came to be VE day—four days after the signing of the surrender of Germany—which Churchill had undertaken would signal preparations for the next election. Attlee had a hand in drafting the formal letter which Churchill sent him on the continuation of the government. But Attlee was overruled by his own party executive meeting in Blackpool which recommended an immediate election and withdrawal from coalition. Bevin and Dalton wanted to keep a coalition but doubted if the full party conference would endorse it. The Labour party's reply was telephoned to the Prime Minister on 21 May and the coalition was broken up two days later.

Chapter three
Strategy and mobilization

Churchill's personal direction of British strategy in the war against Germany before the United States was compelled to join gave a special emphasis to the application of scientific techniques, and an uplift to national morale which sustained the country in its time of greatest peril, when invasion seemed imminent and regular bombing impossible to avoid. The coalition followed in his train. Churchill made himself his own Minister of Defence, and the other ministers in his government thought it wise to leave him to enjoy this role.

The management of war in coalition through his leadership raised the status of military intelligence, and allowed a generation of young people to indulge in a passion for methods of organization which placed a premium on devolved authority and autonomy. Radio communication brought all theatres of war within the scope of the Prime Minister's direction, and the monitoring of enemy radio messages—either centrally in Britain itself or locally in the field of battle—was a major contribution to strategic planning. Like Hitler himself, or like Stalin after 1941, Churchill for the first two or three years of the war kept a tight personal rein on all his commanders in the field; but unlike either of these leaders, he thought through each move in a kind of permanently rolling seminar of advisers, colleagues, and subordinates. His interminable meetings and idiosyncratic working habits with what he called his 'secret circle' were nearly all exercises in persuasion by argument. He very rarely acted in defiance of the advice tendered by his chiefs of staff.

The principal organizations in preparing intelligence, developing weapons, and providing liaison with allies or between forces had opportunities for enterprise and experiment which were directly derived from the knowledge of the right networks to employ in order to reach the 'secret circle'. The young and the intelligent in staff or advisory posts saw innumerable examples of applied communications theory. They lived in a world of messages—the constant tick of the teleprinter and the abbreviated vocabulary of telegraphese—but in situations where the meaning was conveyed by admission to various levels of discourse. Quite frequently individuals or groups working alongside each other were ignorant of each other's business. Formal rank in military terms had to give way to authority in technical expertise or confidence in privileged knowledge.

The mobilization of special units has often been regarded as an exploitation of British manners in creating clubs with membership by invitation only. The merchant banks of the City and Balliol College, Oxford, were the 'old boy network' of the Special Operations Executive; the senior common rooms of Cambridge provided mathematicians for the Government Code and Cipher School. Recruitment was conducted through friends and colleagues whose loyalty was unquestioned. A danger seemed to lie in allowing Churchill himself to indulge in too great a reliance on similar methods. One of the principal achievements in persuasion on his accesion to power was that he accepted the War Cabinet Secretariat and resisted the temptation to create a 'private army' at the centre of affairs, although he did bring with him from the Admiralty his own statistical section, with Cherwell to give special scientific advice. Just before suceeding to the premiership he had hoped as chairman of the military co-ordinating committee to be a sort of 'supreme controller' with a separate secretariat of his own. Hastings Ismay appears to have convinced him that the machinery for running the war already existed[1].

In finding appropriate marriages between communications technology and British social habits, the government in the first year of coalition was strikingly dependent on what had gone before. The political character of Churchill's government was a subtle amalgam of the legacy of previous decisions and his own distinctive contribution. The strategic choices which he faced were limited by the surrender of France and the entry into the war of Italy, which hampered British operations in the Mediterranean. Mussolini, who was waiting for his more favourable moment to bring Italy into the fight, thought that the German defeat of the French was the most auspicious occasion, and postponed his declaration of war until 10 June 1940. Churchill began his supreme command of British interests with the German army and air force threatening attack from France across the English Channel, but he was soon faced with Italian forces moving eastwards through Tripolitania and Cyrenaica towards Egypt, as well as from Abyssinia towards the British colonies of Somaliland, Kenya and the Sudan.

Churchill's power as a strategist depended on decisions already taken in weapons production. He was in no position to play for time and to wait until his resources had increased. It was precisely the critical situation which placed a premium on scientific inventiveness, not only in developing new weapons such as radar, but also and even more significantly, in planning the best use of what was available. Nearly all the strategic achievements of 1940-41 were products of economy of effort, particularly in the deployment of fighter squadrons during the Battle of Britain when Dowding depended on the interception of German radio messages.

The principal assets—insularity and the protection of the seas—were made even more valuable by two incomparable pieces of good fortune. In the first place, German agents who landed in Britain to spy on military activities were either weak or easily 'bent' into working as double agents by British authorities. Germany was deprived of good intelligence from behind the British lines and also at the same time deliberately fed with false information. By the beginning of 1941 the British security services began to hope that through the double agents they did in fact control the German system[2]. In the second place, British air superiority in day-time from 1941 to 1944 deprived the Germans of a regular air reconnaisance system. German intelligence did not use air photographs to anything like the same extent as did its opponents. Only in the final stages of the war did the Germans recover a reconnaisance ability by the use of jet aircraft. Without these two additional benefits to British insularity it seems doubtful whether the secret of the British decipherment of German codes would have been so successfully kept. Churchill's greatest strategic inheritance—the cryptanalyst's break into codes using various versions of the German Enigma machine—preceded his accession to power by only a few weeks. The earliest German signals on Enigma machines, first read by the Poles in 1931, were translated by the Government Code and Cipher School at Bletchley Park in April 1940.

Churchill's government and type of war management had an impact on the political experience of the nation in two principal ways. First, his zest for war and his personal patronage of scientific invention suceeded in creating a spirit of inquiry to test the effectiveness of alternative strategies by empirical methods. No part of the war machine was safe from his imperious requests, his intervention in appointments, or even when the mood caught him, his personal presence on the spot. He loved to travel and to inspect. The Chiefs of Staff were not always happy about his direct access to 'raw intelligence' such as the messages deciphered at Bletchley Park, and feared that he might 'form his own opinions'[3]. But they had to accept that the technology of the war carried imperatives in terms of skilled personnel and new devices which rapidly outpaced their own pre-war preparations. Even if the whole question of assessing the potential of atomic research were discounted, there was still sufficient scope to create opportunities for a generation of young intellectuals whose services proved essential. The cryptanalysts at Bletchley Park were matched by equally hard-headed groups of intelligence officers in the field. The scientists at the research stations had their counterparts in the signal technicians and transport improvisors on active service.

The presence of Americans in British organizations after December 1941 and the regular intermixing of senior staff in the two countries had the effect of underlining how much British official circles had become accustomed to an injection of scientific thinking. Complaints that scientific officers in the Civil Service had never been properly paid or highly regarded were at last heard and steps taken to reconsider their position. What the Americans lacked at the beginning of 1942 was of course not resources, but the rapidly accumulated experience of how to evaluate and distribute intelligence about the enemy.

Second, Churchill's style of management with its fine rhetoric of appeals to the people did not pitch ideology against ideology in a deliberately provocative manner, but sought to defeat Fascism with the simple faiths of old-fashioned nationalism. Insularity and national identity were embodied in the coalition. Again conscription had already been accepted in 1939; it was part of Churchill's strategic inheritance—the people were prepared to fight, however reluctantly and with whatever resignation. The coalition's contribution to national resolve was a cartharsis for the fruitless disputes of the 1930s. The war when it came was so clearly not the kind of struggle which had been feared for so long; it was neither the stalemate of the trenches nor rapid destruction by aerial bombardment. But it could not be ignored. The all-party government symbolized the acceptance of the need to face the enemy.

Intelligence and planning

Churchill managed the military affairs of the government in a manner that gave prominence to technical discussions of scientific appraisal in which other members of the War Cabinet were not usually involved. The marriage of scientific intelligence and strategic planning under the Prime Minister's personal direction stemmed in part from the special circumstances of Britain's isolation after the fall of France in June 1940 and in part from Churchill's own determination to be his own Minister of Defence enjoying direct relationships with the Chiefs of Staff and with commanders in the field. Churchill's predominance over his minsterial colleagues whenever strategic questions were decided was the product of the trust placed in him as one of the principal opponents of the National government's policy of appeasement, and the advocate in the House of Commons of rearmament against Hitler. His return to power after a long exclusion from office—he was not a minister between the Conservatives' failure to win the General Election in May 1929 and the formation of Chamberlain's War Cabinet in September 1939—gave him a zest for applying the 'offensive' approach which he had so long embodied. Churchill enjoyed the prospect of managing military affairs. He knew that the parliamentary coup which had brought him to power guaranteed at least initially a rallying of parliamentary support behind a personal leadership. The Chiefs of Staff were aware that the price of his coalition would be his constant direct interference in operational questions. The military professionals had to do what they could to protect their own judgements from the Prime Minister's marauding activities.

Hastings Ismay, who as Secretary of the Committee of Imperial Defence became head of the military side of the War Cabinet Secretariat at the outbreak of war, acted as liaison between the Prime Minister and the professional heads of the armed services. He was recognized as the chief staff officer to the Prime Minister as Minister of Defence, and minutes from Churchill to the Chiefs of Staff went through his office. He became an additional member of the Chiefs of Staff Committee. Throughout the war he worked extremely long hours, often sixteen a day, standing in the awkward role of the mediator between the Prime Minister and his commanders. Although decisions were usually finalized in the Chiefs of Staffs Committee, a great deal of the discussion of basic options had taken place through Ismay's personal contacts. The translation of Churchill's wishes into administrative action depended on Ismay's skill. Ismay, for example, urged upon those generals who wanted to establish a rapport with the Prime Minister that they should 'write him a long private letter, telling him of your hopes and fears more fully and more freely than is possible in a telegram or even an official letter'. In the summer of 1941 when Churchill was particularly exercised about the need to appoint commanders with the right 'offensive' approach, and when he ordered a number of dismissals and reshuffles, Ismay was closely involved in smoothing the paths of personal relations and protecting the administrative machine from damage.

Other Cabinet ministers from time to time objected to their

exclusion from some of the main lines of communication. Churchill got into the habit not only of having direct exchanges between himself and commanders in the field which he failed to convey to his colleagues, but also of calling special *ad hoc* meetings on technical questions from which stenographers were excluded and of which no record was kept. His own insistence on giving authority for action only by the written word was not matched with a scrupulous concern for copying his instructions to other parties who might claim a right to know. The three service ministers were sometimes placed in a difficult position because they were not fully appraised of the latest discussions.

But Churchill also had the benefit of his own private statistical branch under Cherwell who brought Roy Harrod from Oxford to be the branch's principal economist. That branch analysed and presented to the Prime Minister any statistical information he wanted. Harrod returned to Oxford early in 1942 but was still consulted from time to time by Cherwell who belonged to the same college, Christ Church. Cherwell's surviving papers show that his staff often prepared memoranda which were never submitted formally to the Prime Minister, although their contents may well have been passed by word of mouth.

The special circumstances of Britain's position after the fall of France placed a premium on the cultivation of scientific invention. Both the defence of the British Isles against German aggression and the possibility of mounting any offensive against the weakest points of German control over Europe required an effective use of air power. Churchill's predilection for private meetings on weapons technology was not a suddenly acquired form of self-indulgence but the product of a long fascination with improving the means of warfare. One of his delights in the scientific advice of Cherwell, whom he had first met at Eaton Hall in 1921, was the latter's ability to combine both military and civilian questions for scientific analysis. During the 1930s in his country home at Chartwell, Churchill had discussed the potential in certain lines of research for promoting air power, such as the development of radar. He first took up flying in 1912 in connection with the formation of a Royal Naval Air Service, and had visited Germany with Cherwell in 1932 to study the growth of German air power. From that time onwards he was in the vanguard of those urging the British government to invest in building up the RAF. He and Cherwell (then Lindemann) were urging the Prime Minister to set up a special CID sub-committee on air research in 1934 when the Air Ministry was at the same time inviting Sir Henry Tizard to undertake a scientific survey of air defence. Churchill became a member of the new CID committee in 1935. One of the greatest disappointments of this participation was Baldwin's refusal in July 1936 to accept the arguments for air rearmament advanced by Churchill's deputation.

The dominant questions in Churchill's technical discussions were always what was operationally feasible, given the shortages of men and materials, and what was operationally effective, given the danger of wasting scarce resources. Scientific thinking was applied both to extending what was feasible and to proving what had been effective. It is not surprising that what became known as 'operational research' is a direct scientific product of Britain's 'year alone' in the fight against Germany. Sir Solly Zuckerman found the first mention of the term 'operational research' in the record of discussions over dinner in a club of scientists in November 1941,[5] but by that date both the idea and the practice were well established. In August 1940 P. M. S. Blackett from the Cavendish Laboratory at Cambridge had gathered together a group of scientists to study the operational problems in making the best use of gun-laying radar sets on behalf of the Army's anti-aircraft batteries.[6]

Not surprisingly the first systematic use of 'operational research' was to test the value of air power. Bomber Command set up an operational research section in September 1941 to study the results of each air raid over Germany from the evidence supplied by air reconnaissance. Churchill had his own small parallel investigating section in the form of analyses provided by a member of his statistical section. The important step in this form of applied science was the shift from analysing destruction to identifying targets for future action. The work of two eminent scientists who applied their minds to this field, J. D. Bernal and Solly Zuckerman, exemplified the shift from defence to the offensive. They began working on the effects of blast caused by bombing under the auspices of the Civil Defence Research Committee of the Ministry of Home Security which wanted to know how to protect civilians at home. This analysis led them into what became known as the British Bombing Survey Unit, an instrument which could then be extended to work wherever Allied bombers were in action. They were invited by Mountbatten in the Spring of 1942 to become scientific advisers to the Chief of Combined Operations, and Zuckerman's work henceforward was directed towards devising bombing programmes. In that capacity Zuckerman co-operated closely with RAF operational research personnel which had by that date been appointed in the Middle East and Mediterranean. His bombing plan for the capture of the island of Pantelleria in

May 1943 was the complete justification of the mathematical probability techniques which he had devised in assessing destruction?

Questions of feasibility and effectiveness were direct consequences of the acute shortages which plagued British strategic planning until the American war production programmes got under way in 1942-3. Even then the Allies were not able to summon up sufficient shipping space and assault landing craft for the invasions which they wished to mount. When Churchill first took charge of British armament planning, he gave priority to the manufacture of aircraft—the key weapon in both defence and offence—but as the threat of a direct German attack on the British Isles receded, he was compelled to devote more attention to the interests of the Army and Navy.

The basic dilemma of the Prime Minister and his Chiefs of Staff, was the allocation of resources between the two areas apart from the British Isles in which British interests were most vulnerable to attack, the Middle East and the Far East. The choices to be made in this disposition of force were rendered more problematic by the closure of the Suez Canal to transport supply ships after the fall of France and the Italian entry into the war. The distances between London, Cairo and Singapore were too great to make any rapid adjustments of reinforcement. German control of the heartland of Western Europe gave Hitler the advantage of swift internal lines of communication. British strategic thinking was always tempted to give pride of place to mounting a Balkan offensive—to attack Germany through the area where Hitler attracted little sympathy but where Rumania guaranteed him a continental supply of oil— and to regaining complete control of the Mediterranean.

Churchill and his military colleagues also inherited a commitment to wage war against the enemy in Europe by economic means. The idea of blockading European ports was a well-established convention of strategy based on sea power, and the Committee on Imperial Defence had prepared before the war to set up a Ministry of Economic Warfare. This department came into being as soon as war was declared, taking with it the 'industrial intelligence centre' which had been run by Churchill's friend, Desmond Morton. But as the war progressed, the definition of economic warfare was extended to include all kinds of attacks on industrial potential. 'Operational research' was added to the department's armoury when a unit was created to interpret air reconnaissance photographs taken over Germany in order to make estimates of the damage done to German factories by Bomber Command.

What Churchill and his commanders achieved by 1942 was the

marriage of military intelligence from all sources with strategic planning for all those services, symbolized in the co-operation between two key institutions which Ismay's secretariat maintained, the Joint Intelligence Committee and the Joint Planning Staff. These two organizations presented their proposals to the Chiefs of Staffs Committee. Ismay had himself in 1936, when he was appointed Deputy Secretary of CID, spotted the weaknesses in joint planning which failed to bring together diplomatic reporting and factual intelligence about armament capabil ty. Churchill had succeeded in making himself well informed about British government actions precisely because senior officials were prepared to send him material. From 1934 onwards Desmond Morton fed him with evaluations made by the 'industrial intelligence centre' in preparation for economic warfare; and from 1935 onwards the Foreign Office began letting him see appropriate documentation from diplomatic sources. By the end of 1937 all three service ministries were also using Churchill as a kind of confidential correspondent. He was therefore perfectly familiar with the background to joint planning problems before he came into power. The supreme advantage of a properly articulated Joint Intelligence Committee was that it could bring together not only the directors of intelligence for the three services but also the heads of secret intelligence (MI5 and MI6) and of 'special operations', as well as a representative of the Foreign Office. The Joint Intelligence Staff met their opposite numbers on the Joint Planning Staff very regularly, and the Joint Intelligence Committee met the Chiefs of Staff once a week.

A bonus in addition to this greater sensitivity about intelligence was the availability of knowledge of German actions through the deciphering successes of the Government Code and Cipher School at Bletchley Park. The professionalism of the direction of the war was specifically expressed in the limited circulation of the decrypts from Bletchley Park which provided a steady stream of translations of intercepted enemy messages passed by radio, particularly between the German High Command and its forces in the field. Other forms of interception, such as material from prisoners of war or from resistance movements in occupied territory, were frequently as important in assessing enemy intentions as the miracles of decipherment to emerge from Bletchley Park, but the circulation of the latter was a great boon. After the United States entered the war and Americans were admitted to this 'most reliable source', Churchill's predominance in strategic decisions declined and the system of combined planning added a number of complications to the use of intelligence material. But even when at the height of the invasion of Europe in 1944 the number of people receiving material from Bletchley Park rose to about 4,000, the classification which it received, *Top Secret U*—better known as 'Ultra'—was the mark of confidence. When Churchill called for his latest batch of Ultra intercepts, he had the habit of saying, 'Where are my eggs?' To him the people at Bletchley Park were 'the geese who laid the golden eggs but never cackled.'!

Air intelligence staff in particular were able to pick up a number of very important clues about German weapons technology from Bletchley Park decrypts. Knowledge of German radio beams for air navigation and of rocket propulsion experiments was acquired by tracing evidence first revealed by an intercepted message. R. V. Jones who was in charge of scientific intelligence for the Air Staff has pointed out that he always hesitated to rely on this 'most secret source', but there is no doubt that the planned deception of the enemy by radio messages would not have been feasible without an accurate knowledge of his intentions.

The greatest difficulty of the Chiefs of Staff was to restrain the Prime Minister's own 'offensive mind' when it became attracted by operational proposals that had not come up for consideration through orthodox channels, and when the armed forces themselves were not always happy about the disposition of resources among them. Churchill had ordered that the authentic documents of decipherment should be submitted to him in their original form, without being sifted or digested. All his pre-war experience in opposition had accustomed him to make his own interpretations with the help of a few trusted advisers, not the full apparatus of a high command. There seems little doubt that for the first two years of the coalition, while Churchill was in a leading position as a strategist, his possession of knowledge about enemy difficulties which was derived from 'Ultra' led him to press hard against the judgements of commanders in the field. His dismissal of Wavell and Auchinleck in the Middle East was in part due to his feeling that they were not taking sufficient advantage of the shortages from which German forces under Rommel had suffered. The arguments between Churchill and his commanders were usually about the feasibility and value of particular operations. The Prime Minister developed what they regarded as certain obsessions, such as the need to capture scattered islands; and he for his part thought that one or two commanders lacked drive. Churchill prided himself on making the right appointments, but he was often shown to be wrong, particularly in the Navy which had to take Harwood as commander in the Mediterranean and Edward-Collins in Gibraltar after the dismissal of Sir Dudley North.

The only occasions when his will was thwarted in the making of appointments were when the morale of the high command would have been damaged if he had not acceded to the wishes of the majority. For example, when Sir Dudley Pound died in 1943, Churchill was compelled to accept Admiral Cunningham as his successor in the post of First Sea Lord because the whole body of senior admirals would have resented any other promotion.

The entry of the Americans into the war did not transform the content of the arguments on strategy but raised them to the different plane of combined planning. British scientists were already in touch with research in the United States which was relevant to strategic problems. To a large extent prompted by a desire to benefit from American knowledge on the physics of uranium which was required in laying plans for an atomic bomb, Tizard in September 1940 had led a British mission to Washington with the express purpose of sharing scientific secrets between the two countries. After the mission a scientific office was added to the British Supply Council Secretariat in Washington. By March 1941 scientists on both sides of the Atlantic had proof of the feasibility of a uranium bomb, provided the technical problems of isotope separation could be overcome. By July 1941, the principal scientists in Roosevelt's new Office of Scientific Research and Development were suggesting that the American and British governments should co-operate on a joint project of research into atomic weapons? But at that stage Britain wanted to retain control of an independent initiative. It was indicative of Britain's diminishing power in the Alliance that when the final joint arrangements were made in 1943 to build the atomic bomb the Americans were in the stronger position to dictate terms.

The technical discussions of the Chiefs of Staff after January 1942 took place in the context of a Combined meeting of Chiefs of Staff—of Britain and the United States. Strategic planning was geared to a jointly constructed 'order of battle' on which the campaign against Germany was given priority. Before their entry into the war the American commanders had worked out a 'Germany first' approach in spite of the danger of a Japanese attack in the Pacific, and they found no immediate difficulty in coming to terms with British thinking. Churchill had also at the same time been able to effect an important change in senior appointments on the British side. Sir John Dill, the Chief of the Imperial General Staff, who had had strong differences of opinion with Churchill on the idea of a Balkan offensive and had relinquished his post in December 1941, agreed to join the British delegation to Washington in that month when Churchill met Roosevelt at the ARCADIA conference, and to remain there as the senior British representative on the Combined Chiefs of Staff. His standing in American military circles eased the difficulties in joint planning. Sir Alan Brooke, Dill's successor as Chief of the Imperial General Staff, who in fact had stayed behind in London during the Washington discussions, replaced Sir Dudley Pound, the First Sea Lord, as chairman of the Chiefs of Staff Committee in March 1942 — a crucial step in getting the Chiefs of Staff to smooth over their differences. Pound had been according to Brooke 'like an old parrot asleep on his perch'[10].

The arrival of the Americans did not alter the problems faced by British military planners but presented them with the difficulty of how and where to get the United States engaged. It seemed vital to both Roosevelt and Churchill that the Americans should be seen in the European theatre during 1942. Both leaders were also sure that the only place from which an Allied invasion of Europe could be mounted was the United Kingdom itself. The latter could only provide such a launching site if it were adequately defended both in the air and on the sea. Nearly all the Combined Chiefs of Staffs' work was concerned with how to 'close the ring' around Germany while preparing for and mounting an invasion in Europe.

Gaining success against the Japanese in the Pacific was in fact much closer to the American heart, particularly after the disastrous collapse of the British Empire in the Far East. From February 1942 onwards the hopes of a British return to that theatre of war were extremely dependent on American effort; and from August 1942 when the Americans began to make their first gains, the fears that the United States would be tempted to switch resources away from Europe played an important part in British calculations. The timing of Hitler's invasion of Russia in June 1941 meant that the American commanders joined strategic discussions on Europe just when the principal British debate was about how to draw off some German strength from the Eastern front in order to help their new Soviet allies. The Americans walked straight into the 'Second Front Now' controversy which divided British opinion. The British had been singularly unsuccessful in holding the Germans back by attacking through the Balkans. From the spring of 1941 the whole British war effort in the Middle East was forced onto the defensive. In April 1941 the German Panzer divisions threw the British forces out of Greece, and in May, largely because the British failed to hold an airfield that was crucial to German plans for landing troop carriers, the island of Crete was also lost. With Rommel's attack on British forces in the western desert the whole of the British war effort became centred on the North African coast and on the Eastern Mediteranean. For eighteen months this theatre of war attracted the most attention from British strategic planners. It was precisely the decision to bring American forces into the European war through a joint Anglo-American landing of forces in North Africa (Algeria and Morocco) that led the British to begin to share their 'secret sources' with the Americans. Until the summer of 1942 most of the traffic in secret intelligence had been one way—from the United States to Britain—particularly after the Americans had cracked an important Japanese cipher. Eisenhower's arrival in England in June 1942 as the American general chosen to take charge of the Anglo-American landings marked a new phase in the alliance. When those landings took place under his command in November, strategic planning and intelligence work were brought together on a joint staff basis.

Nearly all British disagreements with the Americans about operational feasibility and effectiveness stemmed from differences over the degree to which the demands for men and materials in the Mediterranean theatre of war could be limited. Americans became suspicious that by using the Mediterranean in 'closing the ring' against Germany, the Allies might indirectly be serving British political interests in the Middle East. These suspicions were strengthened as the American High Command began in 1943 to calculate the likely effects on a European peace settlement of a Soviet advance on the Eastern front.

In calculating how to harass Germany while an invasion of Europe was prepared, each one of the armed forces argued for a different disposition of resources. The Army was awkwardly placed, because it required the support of the Navy and the RAF to launch an invasion. Whatever it put into the Mediterranean reduced its power to invade Western Europe. The Navy wanted all the resources it could acquire to protect the sea lanes of the Atlantic, and to destroy the extremely powerful German battleships which had exposed its weaknesses. It had never quite recovered from the lack of investment and the naval limitation treaties of the inter-war period. The RAF was dominated by the offensive potential of Bomber Command which could strike into enemy territory. A great deal of the strongest disputation was reserved for the argument over whether aeroplanes which were vital to winning the Battle of the Atlantic against the U-boats should be diverted to operations over Germany itself. Scientific and technical questions arose in the context of night bomber sorties to destroy German towns. The Navy objected to the 1,000 bomber raid on Cologne in May 1942. 'Operational research' techniques did not immediately justify this investment of effort.

These differences lost their significance in the life of the coalition after the summer of 1943. By that stage of the war the Prime Minister had himself come to recognize that Britain could only play a junior role after the invasion itself had begun. What he had achieved was the prevention of a premature invasion of the Continent by forces not properly prepared, and the very decision to concentrate on North Africa in 1942 had postponed the accumulation of sufficient material to land a strong enough force outside the Mediterranean in 1943. The key decisions in joint Anglo-American planning were taken at the Casablanca conference in January 1943 when the Combined Chiefs of Staff began preparations for a cross-Channel invasion of France from Britain to take place in the summer of 1944. It was also then agreed that the Allies should harry the Axis by invading Sicily. When the Combined Chiefs of Staff again met in Washington in May 1943 the British won the argument to keep up the pressure in the Mediterranean by organizing an invasion of the Italian mainland. But after the Quebec Conference in August 1943, in spite of the hopes still entertained for a speedy victory in Italy, it was clear that Churchill's personal position as a strategist was declining in importance. The Battle of the Atlantic had been won, or at least reduced to a manageable scale; the plans for a cross-Channel invasion were largely in American hands; the British forces in South-East Asia could not mount the operations they wanted for lack of materials.

The only minister in the coalition to challenge the Prime Minister's strategic preconceptions touched him in a vulnerable spot, but made little impression. Leo Amery, the Secretary of State for India, who like Churchill had been out of office for over ten years, from time to time put forward strategic ideas for the defence of India and the British possessions in the Far East.[11] He was closely associated with Dorman-Smith, the Governor of Burma forced into exile by the Japanese invasion. Churchill was in fact so obsessed with the internal dangers of conceding to the demands of the Indian nationalists that he asked his former principal private secretary, P. J. Grigg, then permanent secretary at the War Office, to read the telegrams exchanged between Amery and the Government of India in order to monitor Amery's actions[12] Amery's strategic ideas received fairly short shrift.

Part of the reason for Churchill's diminished status in Allied planning was his barely disguised irritation with the increasing predominance of the Americans. He seemed to long for a theatre of war in which the British alone could make their mark, as the Eighth Army had done in the western desert in 1942. American suspicions of his interest in Mediterranean operations were based on a feeling that he was seeking a separate road to glory.

Information and management

Peace-time hierarchies in government departments were displaced by the networks created in order to bring scientific intelligence of all kinds to bear on the problems of strategy. The horizontal separation between ministers and officials was broken by vertical lines of communication and 'mixed' committees containing politicians, civil servants and serving officers. The existence of a coalition government which had been expressly formed to give Churchill the supreme command aided the formation of 'private armies' and liaison units which were designed to short-circuit the normal chains of command or to protect special sources of information. Those who felt neglected or ignored complained of treachery or conspiracy. For example, Reith's diary contains accusations and recriminations about the treatment he received as Minister of Works. Harry Crookshank, the Financial Secretary to the Treasury and a senior member of the Conservative Party like his ministerial colleague, Sir Kingsley Wood, Chancellor of the Exchequer, filled his diary for 1942 with complaints that he was underemployed and that 'Kingsley doesn't consult me'. War-time conditions of speedy decisions and rapid changes of mood brought out many latent antagonisms. The networks which were successful were in danger of being overloaded by others trying to share in the success; those which failed to make any impression gathered together the resentful and suspicious. Churchill's leadership exaggerated the differences between good and bad reputations in normal bureaucratic politics; and in war the good and the bad are always on the move. All commanders want to share in the charisma of the good, and to speed the bad onto somebody else's responsibility.

The supremely nationalistic qualities of talented people selecting each other for special tasks gave a distinctive tone to the government apparatus while Britain stood alone and before the presence of Americans in joint planning shifted strategic thinking onto a different plane. It then became necessary to invent the security classification, 'UK eyes only'. But while Churchill enjoyed his unique 'dictator' position both individuals and groups were able to use their influence in the constantly shifting patterns of official appointments to write their own 'terms of reference' and to do their best to invent their own 'job descriptions'. What needed to be done was being redefined, and each 'captain' strove to impose his own perception of need at different levels of the war machine. R. V. Jones, working with MI6 in December 1940, drew up a scheme for a complete 'Scientific Intelligence Service'; Hugh

Trevor-Roper manoeuvred himself inside MI6 to be able to supply all potential users with Bletchley Park decrypts from the German 'Abwehr' instead of working solely within his own organisation. Bureaucratic in-fighting often seemed more important than calculations of political party interest. It is not surprising that the whole tone of official activity in government departments should have begun to change as the long war and the American alliance made Churchill's strategic leadership less important.

The Labour members of the government were always being accused by some of their own party of legitimatizing a form of bureaucratic regulation which gave little representation to the interests of the working classes. They felt particularly vulnerable during the winter of 1940-41 when it looked as if some back-benchers were deliberately trying to raise the accusation of 'MacDonaldism'—a betrayal of Labour interests to a Conservative-dominated 'national government'. From the other side Churchill let it be known that he felt he could rule without their aid. He did not feel that he faced any real challenge in Parliament, at least not until the rise to prominence in 1942 of Sir Stafford Cripps; and even then it seemed highly unlikely that he would be forced out of office, although the loss of Singapore was a major military defeat. Labour Ministers accepted this situation, in spite of the awkward position in which they were occasionally placed by their own party. Some of them were as heavily involved in bureaucratic intrigue as the 'temporary civil service' in science or intelligence. Hugh Dalton, for example, both at the Ministry of Economic Warfare and at the Board of Trade after 1942 delighted in fixing matters outside the normal channels. He even had his own 'temporary civil servant' allies in Hugh Gaitskell and Douglas Jay, prominent young Labour Party men who worked in his ministry.

It is almost impossible in retrospect to reconstruct which member of the government enjoyed particular confidences—the what, when, and why of marrying intelligence and strategy. When nationalism pervades every government action, it is not necessary to explain the connections between all parts of the system in order to secure both loyalty and effectiveness. An amazing number of confidences were sealed with loyalty and dedication. Each individual in the high command learnt not to ask the wrong questions or to invite deliberate deception; spouses sometimes lived together for years without knowing each other's official business. The wife of the commandant of Bletchley Park did not understand why her husband was knighted at the end of the war. The most important feature of the networks of intelligence and specially protected lines of communication was the ability to exercise influence 'without pulling rank'—the authority given to those who could secure easy access to the Prime Minister. When the Civil Service authorities would promote R. V. Jones one grade only to Principal Scientific Officer instead of three grades to Deputy Director, he decided 'not to fight but to depend for my authority on the value of the work I was doing, aided by the general impression that I had at any time only to go to Churchill to ask him to issue appropriate orders'[13].

Compartmentalism was deliberately cultivated. It was necessary at many levels and in many different organizations to design points of 'cut off'—a boundary which isolated one 'community' from another—so that the betrayal of one set of secrets did not lead automatically to the enemy's discovery of another. It was axiomatic in the working of the Special Operations Executive which aided resistance movements in Europe to fight against Nazi occupation that the capture of a secret agent by the enemy meant the information he carried was also lost. Nobody was invulnerable to torture. Although the British Isles were happily free from the imperatives of occupation, it was still necessary to protect information with principles of organization which reflected the dangers to be faced.

It was also important to encourage forms of deliberate deception —how to cover up the tracks of an operation so that it would not be immediately discovered. One of the remarkable successes of the strategic planning apparatus over which Churchill presided was the organization set up to decieve the enemy about the Allies' intentions. Ismay was the link between Churchill and the small unit known as the London Clearing Section under Colonel John Bevan which learnt how to use secret intelligence. Within the scope of this unit came the celebrated management of 'double agents'— those German spies in Britain who had been turned round by the British to send back intelligence to Germany. The British deception managers aided by 'Ultra' had the unparalleled satisfaction of seeing how well their activities sowed seeds of mistrust between the Axis powers. In March 1941, for example, Admiral Cunningham brought the British fleet to defeat the Italians at Matapan with a complete surprise attack, thanks to 'Ultra' intelligence, only to discover by a further monitoring of enemy signals that the Germans thought that the Italians carried traitors in their midst[14].

The supreme expression of vertical links which cut through the normal lines of communication were the 'special liaison units' set up by Group Captain Winterbotham in order to process the distribution of decrypts from Bletchley Park to commanders in the field. The personnel in these units were normally of a very subordinate rank but they had to be trusted to prevent 'leakages' by their superiors. Winterbotham at first chose reliable friends, but as the network of distribution developed, he had to train and indoctrinate new staff. They had to learn how to stop an Air Marshal stuffing 'Ultra' papers into the top of his flying boots. They had to be on guard against any traces of typex paper, the product of ciphering machines, sticking to the soles of their own shoes. Service in a 'special liaison unit' was *par excellence* a frequent exercise in how to use influence without enjoying rank.

Churchill encouraged a sense of 'family' among the staff of the 'special liaison units'. When he was travelling around the different threatres of war he expected to be serviced by 'his people' with the 'Ultra' papers[15]. This intimacy led him to respect the decision of individual officers, such as Wing-Commander Crawshaw who declined to run the risk of carrying 'Ultra' papers to the Prime Minister on the Italian front, and at the same time to treat such officers with a courtesy and personal attention quite beyond the bounds of their expectations. The sense of 'family' was an extension of admission to the 'secret circle'. The lines around 'secret intelligence' were drawn very arbitrarily. None of Churchill's private secretaries were on the 'Ultra' list of knew precisely what the Prime Minister was receiving in 'yellow boxes'. Even Jacob, the Military Secretary of the War Cabinet, was not formally appraised of Ultra itself[16]. The link with the Chiefs of Staff was always supplied by Ismay.

But within 'the circle' scientific intelligence provoked 'family' divisions in the form of rivalries between the armed services, because the strategic problems which the high command had to face were conceived differently by each service when weapons were in short supply. As Ronald Lewin has shown in his study of the impact of Bletchley Park work on strategic decision-making[17], the commanders in the field frequently received 'the message'— prior knowledge of what the enemy intended to do—but missed 'the meaning'—the critical factor in the success or failure of the planned operation. In 1941 Freyberg defending Crete failed to notice that the enemy needed to capture an airfield quickly; Wavell facing Rommel's Africa Korps in the western desert assumed the enemy would build up a supply system along the coast. Errors of tactics arose from strategic preconceptions. No matter how well informed the individual commander might be, he tended to follow the traditional habits of his service.

The three service ministers in the government—Alexander, Sinclair, Margesson (and then Grigg)—presented the cases of their departments at the appropriate meetings, but do not appear to have made any major contributions to the course of the debate. The 'family' arguments revolved around the Chiefs of Staff. Indeed, each of the services made its own arrangements to consider both the interpretation of German decrypts and the application of scientific advice. Unlike the other two departments, the Admiralty was itself an operational centre issuing orders directly to fleets on the high seas, and from the beginning a separate naval section was maintained at Bletchley Park. The Navy dissociated itself from the 'special liaison units' which Winterbotham organized for the Army and RAF. It insisted on channeling all information through its own Operational Intelligence Centre in Whitehall. Scientific advice was also divided on a service basis. Each ministry made its own arrangements to secure appropriate technical expertise in weapon developments and it ran its own research establishments. The principal research establishment to escape to some extent outside the departmental structure was at Whitchurch, where a secret station under a Ministry of Supply cover enjoyed a direct relationship with the Prime Minister through his adviser, Cherwell[18]. This establishment specialized in the design of special weapons.

Scientific advice on strategic problems tended to divide the Chiefs of Staff whenever they had to consider using the British Isles as an offensive base against Germany. Differences between the services in other theatres of war were more easily reconciled, particularly after the American entry into the war when the feasibility of operations depended on joint staff decisions. Questions arising from the policy of 'closing the ring' around Europe or from plans for large-scale invasion did not involve British personnel alone. But the position of the British Isles both before and after the American entry was clearly something which required the careful attention of the British high command. Not only were these islands the obvious springboard for an invasion of Germany, but also the sanctuary of many European 'governments in exile' which hoped to return to power in the wake of the Allied armies.

The crucial strategic importance of the British Isles also emphasized the value of high morale of its civilian population which was always vulnerable to German air attack. Hitler's 'secret weapon' — the rocket-propelled pilotless bomber first fired by the Germans in October 1942 — which began to be treated as a serious threat by Air Intelligence in March 1943,[19] was deliberately designed to attack British civilian morale. It was surprising in view of the political importance of effective defence against all forms of air attack that a larger number of ministers in the Government did not try to participate in the technical discussions which tried to resolve difference between the three services. The survival of the country depended both on guaranteeing the sea lanes to protect imported food supplies and on preventing destruction by aerial bombard-ment. In fact, some of the key decisions were reached in 'mixed committees' or simply in *ad hoc* meetings chaired by the Prime Minister.

The principal area of dispute in which both science and secret intelligence played a leading part was what Churchill called 'the Wizard War'—a term initially applied to defending Britain from the air but then applied to the strategic air offensive against Germany. Technical questions were uppermost in Churchill's meetings with the Chiefs of Staff because the evidence of air reconnaisance frequently showed that 'precision bombing' against military targets was rarely effective. Striking against Germany from the air there-fore involved estimating the consequences of killing civilians; just as planning the invasion of Europe meant calculating the effects of killing the civilian population under Nazi occupation. Disputes on the value of strategic bombing became more acrimonious in 1942 as new aircraft came into service for the first time with improved navigational equipment—Stirlings, Halifaxes and Lancasters—and as the newly appointed 'chief' of Bomber Command, Arthur Harris, began to press his arguments for massive raids on German towns. A comparable argument ensued in 1943-4 when the Combined Chiefs of Staff decided to use heavy bombers against the enemy's transportation system in France prior to the planned Allied invasion and thus endangered many French lives.

Nearly all subsequent comments on this area of dispute have concentrated on the dramatic confrontation between Cherwell as Churchill's principal scientific adviser and Tizard as the principal scientific adviser to the Air Ministry. Although only head of the Prime Minister's statistical section, Cherwell had such a close relationship with Churchill that he had to be treated as almost a member of the Government. His standing underlined the fact that even ministerial status did not automatically carry influence in the counsels of the coalition. What mattered was access to 'the secret circle' and allies within it. The tensions generated by Cherwell were of long standing. He had been introduced into the secret research on radio direction finding during the 1930s when Churchill had been admitted into these matters, and had even then caused some discord among the other scientists involved, such as Tizard, A. V. Hill, and P. M. S. Blackett. Cherwell was aware of the factions which had grown up around the issues of 'science and war'. When he achieved his position of influence close to Churchill in May 1940, he said, 'a lot of my old friends have come sniffing around'[20].

The first confrontation took place early in the life of the coalition

—June 1940. Cherwell supported the contention that the Germans had by that time invented a radio device which would guide their bombers onto the target by means of a navigational beam known as 'Knickebein'. The Air Staff declined proposals that the RAF itself should adopt a radar guidance system, and Tizard as their adviser denied the feasibility of such a device. But in a special meeting Churchill was convinced by the evidence presented by R. V. Jones that the Germans in fact had such an aid to navigation and ordered counter-measures to be taken immediately. This order was of crucial importance in the Battle of Britain. Tizard resigned from his position at the Air Ministry as a recognition of this error of judgement.

A debate then ensued in the press and in Parliament during 1940-42 on the need for the better application of scientific methods to both war technology and war management. To some extent the public pronouncements of eminent scientists reflected the degree to which they belonged to the faction formed against Cherwell. Many scientists thought that Cherwell had too easy an access to the Prime Minister and was therefore too influential. The Government responded to the debate by establishing the Scientific Advisory Committee in October 1940 under the chairmanship of Lord Hankey. This committee which was given very general terms of reference was composed of representatives from existing scientific organizations, three from different branches of the Royal Society and three secretaries of the government research councils (Department of Scientific and Industrial Research, Agricultural Research Council and Medical Research Council). This committee structure brought together two separate branches of the science establishment—university science and government research establishments. Before the outbreak of war university scholars had tended to regard the staff of the research establishments as second-rate, but with the great expansion of defence-related research inside government, the status of such staff was completely transformed by the infusion of a new talented personnel. Yet any idea of recognizing this transformation by making a new set of consultative councils was frustrated by the presence of the Scientific Advisory Committee. The 'official members' who composed it were hostile to any change. Scientists were compelled to rely on informal networks and influential consultants.

Cherwell and Tizard clashed again in 1942 over the effectiveness of the strategic air offensive. Cherwell maintained that German war production could be crippled if greater resources were given to Bomber Command; Tizard, then advising the Ministry of Aircraft Production, supported the case for providing more aircraft to concentrate on the destruction of U-boats in the Atlantic. The same sense of personal rivalry persisted in the making of plans for post-war defence research. This time from October 1943 onwards, Tizard was drawing up a scheme for a 'defence policy research committee' and for a 'government scientific adviser'. He had an opportunity to put his ideas into practice in December 1944 when the Chiefs of Staff allowed him to counter German rocket attacks through a Joint Technical Warfare Committee. But Cherwell got the Prime Minister's permission to make his own personal report on 'post-war R. & D. for the services' and after the collapse of the coalition in May 1945 to set up a Cabinet Committee on Defence Research.

The 1942 controversy on the strategic air offensive in fact led to the creation of one of the most distinguished 'mixed committees' of the war, the Prime Minister's Anti- U Boat Warfare Committee from November 1942 to April 1943.[21] This committee consisted of the service ministers, the Chiefs of Staff, the Minister of Transport, the Commander of Coastal Command, and a number of distinguished scientists. One of the latter, P. M. S. Blackett, claimed subsequently that the operations supervised by this committee finally put operational research 'on the map'. Coastal Command was both statistically and scientifically controlled.

To the benefit of the political life of the nation the application of scientific method was frequently made through precisely this kind of 'mixed' apparatus, and the pursuit of scientific research became much more closely associated with the development of appropriate teams. Scientists learnt the value of organization and, perhaps even more important, the need for regular consultation between different organizations. The Cavendish Laboratory before 1939 had been relatively stable in size, and the style of conducting scientific research was in small intimate groups. But the recruitment of scientists from universities to government establishments led to a much more elaborate set of team methods. Improvisation because of shortages also led to greater co-operation between colleagues. Sir Harrie Massey has recorded that by 1943 'it was almost impossible to secure an additional working second-hand ammeter, let alone more advanced electrical instruments'[22].

Perhaps the key to appreciating what the displacement of peace-time methods meant lies in the work of research establishments and special teams which practised both 'compartmentalism' and 'network management'. The security and effectiveness of scientific experiment required something of the 'cut off' between units normally pursued in clandestine intelligence or subversive operations. But once ideas had emerged, they had to be channeled in directions where the findings seemed relevant.

The development of radar and of the atomic bomb—the most important of all the scientific additions to weapons technology—was undertaken with a happy mixture of university scientists and government establishments. University men were at first irritated by the bureaucratic procedures of the civil service. By 1935, for example, the National Physical Laboratory had no suitable measuring equipment to test Cherwell's hypothesis about the infra-red emission in aircraft exhausts, and was obliged to ask the Clarendon Laboratory to do the trials for them. R. V. Jones says that an officer in the Royal Aircraft Establishment telephoned him to request him to bring a length of glass tubing on his next visit, because the stores procedure would not be capable of providing the tubing on time. But gradually government establishments learnt how to improvise. The Air Ministry Research Establishment at Bawdsey provided Watson-Watt with freedom to recruit appropriate staff for the development of radar. Although marred by differences between British and American teams, the pursuit of atomic research was similarly organized with freedom to recruit on a confidential basis. By the end of 1943 British scientists saw that their work was not indispensable to the building of an atomic bomb, and that they should send as many key personnel as possible to the United States in order to acquire experience in the organization which the Americans had established[23]. It was clear that scientific research on this scale demanded a knowledge of the problems faced by large teams. The planning of post-war capacity for the manufacture of atomic energy arose from this American experience.

It would be a mistake to attribute all such achievements in organization to the special features of Churchill's leadership or to the patriotic unity of the coalition, although both phenomena greatly affected the outcome of the applied science brought into use. It looks sometimes as if the abrasive characters in committee confrontations were copying the calculated spitefulness of Oxford Senior Common Rooms. At other times the drama seems to stem from a conflict between the basic institutions of the military strategist and the procedure of 'disciplined observation' by the scientist. There was a tendency after the war to suppress memories of the bitterness which surrounded the controversies on the strategic air offensive. As the official historians noted later, no medal was struck to reward those taking part in the bombing and few references to their achievement were given in Churchill's memoirs. Yet Bomber Command's operations over Germany exacted a grave toll in the loss of life—55,888 officers and other ranks killed. Both the drama of the disputes it caused and the suppression of its achievements stemmed in part from the autonomy which it had acquired under Arthur Harris's leadership. The Air Staff found if extremely difficult to control this enterprise after the summer of 1942. The Casablanca Conference in January 1943 had endorsed a joint Anglo-American bombing attack for 'the progressive destruction of German military, industrial and economic systems and the undermining of the morale of the German people'. Scientific arguments could not make many inroads on this general directive.

What mattered in the life of the coalition was that a number of scientists and intelligence officers had thrown off the inhibitions of peace-time organization to build up a network of advice and analysis alongside both Ministers and Chiefs of Staff. Experience at this level could never be ignored; it provided a basis for confidence in the adaptability of institutions for organizing research. There was no sugestion in scientific circles that the administrative apparatus had not stood up well to the demands laid upon it. It now seems entirely appropriate that so many of the scientists involved in war-time research had between the wars taken an interest in the developments of experimental biology, and indeed in what became known as 'social biology'. Scientific thinking was accustomed to ecology, population control and eugenics. It was a fairly easy step from biophysics to studying the effects of bombing. The scientists involved had the satisfaction of working closely with serving officers through the research establishments in understanding tactical questions. The need for air defence and economy in the use of fighters in 1940 had encouraged ways of thinking about radar which stressed the conservation of resources. The liaison between the scientists and the men who undertook the operations was sufficiently close to give a strong sense of achievement on both sides. As Churchill told R. V. Jones, 'your name will open all doors!'[24] The reputations made were not easily lost.

Conscription and manpower

What worried those in authority was not the adaptability of the administration, which they proved was fairly flexible, but the continued consent of the governed to the controls of mobilization after prolonged exposure to the psychological effects of combat. They wanted to know about the political consequences of conscription to the armed forces and the direction of the labour force in weapons production. They realized that in some sense a managed economy meant an extension of the body politic. Each citizen had his taxes paid by his employer under Pay As You Earn, and his freedom of movement curtailed by the statutes regulating national service, which also gave the government power to change the categories and age of call-up. Ministers and officials when they paused to think about these administrative controls asked themselves the obvious questions—does war engender radical political opinions? At what point of exhaustion will the people panic?

Such questions were more easily answered on the 'home front' than in theatres of war overseas. The morale of population in the big towns in Britain was much more quickly assessed than the preparedness of the forces abroad. While the country 'stood alone' before the entry of Russia and then the United States into the struggle, the heat of the battle seemed very close. It was natural to pay attention to the psychological effects of air raids and the threat of invasion rather than consider the morale of those called to arms. The country's survival after the 'blitz' and the extension of the war to all parts of the globe in 1941-2 transformed the context in which these political questions were asked.

The initial moves made by the government to safeguard civilian morale were both hesitant and incompetent. The Ministry of Information embodied all the doubts of the 'governing classes' about the resilience of the civilian population. That department employed such a large number of middle-class intellectuals in its assessment of home morale and in its decisions on propaganda that if often misjudged the mood of the people and put out posters and pamphlets written in an inappropriate language. The Ministry's publicity campaign sometimes revealed more about the obsessions of its staff than about popular belief. It entered into silly debates on whether it was necessary to demonstrate that the nation as a whole would suffer from a German victory, not just the propertied classes; or whether it was possible to get professional footballers to counteract Nazi propaganda. It was only gradually able to formulate the rule: 'the whiter the collar, the less the assurance'[25]. What distressed the intelligentsia did not move the mass of the people.

The government in 1940-41 were naturally reluctant to abandon 'the volunteer principle'—that the best service is provided willingly and without compulsion. The civil defence services and the Home Guard which bore the brunt of German bomber attacks on major cities were largely manned by volunteers; and the emegency ambulance, first aid, canteen and rehousing services depended on women's voluntary groups and the Red Cross. It was a major break with tradition to contemplate directing labour into part-time police, fire service and civil defence jobs.

But in the winter of 1941-2 the government was compelled to

'shake out' labour from whatever source it could—factories, civil service and even the armed forces. It became clear in the first attempts at a 'manpower survey' that the War Cabinet could not avoid taking drastic action if it were to satisfy both Churchill's priority for the building of long-range bombers and the Chiefs of Staff's desire to send more troops overseas. The 'manpower crisis' of 1941-2 was identified and tackled before there was evidence that the United States was about to become a belligerent, and the discipline which it imposed paid great dividends in the course of the following year.

The crucial decision announced in December 1941 before the Japanese attack on Pearl Harbour was to conscript unmarried women between the ages of twenty and thirty. The basic calculation was that it would only be possible to send more men into the armed forces if women who had hitherto remained in their homes could be brought into the working population. The Cabinet recognized that this decision was fraught with political difficulties. Such a shift in the structure of the working population would make it extremely important to make proper provision for demobilization, as soon as the prospect of diminishing the labour force in weapons production could be contemplated. Mobilization and demobilization became major items on the Cabinet's agenda.

By mid-1943 the government had succeeded in bringing more than 2 million women into the total working population. At this stage of the war the British economy was at full stretch in support of the war effort; both the armed forces and the war production system were geared for the planned invasion of Europe. There are a number of indices which present the bare facts of this situation.

Redistribution of Manpower (millions)

	mid-1939	mid-1943	mid-1945
Males	14.7	15.0	14.9
Females	5.1	7.3	6.7
Total working population	19.8	22.3	21.6
Armed forces and civil defence	0.6	5.1	5.2
Supplies and equipment for the forces	1.3	5.1	3.8
Manufactures for export	1.0	0.2	0.4
Manufactures for the home market	4.5	2.4	2.6
Other industries and services	11.1	9.4	9.5
Unemployed	1.3	0.1	0.1

Source: Tables in Hancock and Gowing, *British War Economy* (1949) pp. 352, 357.

A parallel set of decisions which underlined the seriousness of the manpower problem was the deliberate diversion of resources from the manufacture of consumer goods for the working population, and a limitation on imports. The full force of rationing in food, clothes, furniture and petrol was felt by the average household during 1942. By that stage of the war effort the Ministry of Information believed that the public preferred to accept a system of rationing than to be asked to reduce consumption voluntarily. The government was nevertheless obliged to order the Ministry to launch a fuel economy campaign when back-bench Tory MPs refused to support a scheme for rationing coal, gas and electricity. There was a clear connection between the widespread acceptance of austerity and the popular vision of victory on the battlefield. Brendan Bracken gave his last monthly report to Cabinet on home morale in November 1942 just after the second battle of El Alamein. 'We must stop appealing to the public or lecturing it,' he wrote, 'one makes it furious, the other resentful.'[26]

The sacrifice of the civilian population in 1942-3 can be easily demonstrated in the basic statistics of the government's total management of the economy.

| | Overseas Trade | | Consumer's | Dwellings |
	Volume of imports (Indices 1938=100)	Volume of exports	expenditure (at 1938 prices £ million)	built (thousands)
1938	100	100	4304	362
1939	97	94	4307	359
1940	94	72	3888	212
1941	82	56	3715	48
1942	70	36	3669	13
1943	77	29	3602	13
1944	80	31	3711	8
1945	62	46	3922	18

Sources: Tables 53, 142 and 186 of *Statistical Digest of the War,* (1951).

The austerity experienced at home and the direct application of manpower planning had their effects on the government's discussion of the armed forces themselves. Attention was switched from the home front to questions of political importance in the handling and posting of military personnel. The expansion of the scope of the war in 1942 and the pressures exerted on the troops by the domestic economy working at full stretch produced noticeable changes in the experience of active service. John Colville, for example, a private secretary from the Diplomatic Service at No. 10 Downing Street, when Churchill came to power, has recalled the contrast between the conditions he experienced in sailing out to South Africa for training as a RAF pilot in January 1942 and those a year later on his return home. On the mess deck during the passage out, he was subject to both discomfort and harsh discipline, while the officers were dancing on 'A' Deck to the sound of the ship's orchestra; as a pilot officer on the passage back, he found that all ranks were subjected to the same 'equally dreary austerity'.[27]

The authorities did not immediately anticipate that the scientific management techniques which they were prepared to use at home could also be applied in a somewhat similar fashion to the problems of deployment in the battlefield. Although not so intellectually attractive as the puzzles of 'operational research', one of the achievements of the medical corps in the armed forces—partly perhaps after 1942 as a result of American examples—was an official recognition that different forms of battle had different psychological effects. Applied psychology was employed to deal with 'combat exhaustion'. Techniques were developed to select appropriate personnel for special operations. It was agreed that the intensity and duration of exposure to gunfire reduced the individual infantryman's effectiveness. The notion of 'shell-shock' was abandoned as a general term to cover all nervous cases.[28]

The government had by 1942 reached the point of reconsidering how to recruit and train the numbers of officers required to command the expanded armed forces. The War Office instead of relying on family connexion and the intuitive good sense of serving officers in recommending names for promotion agreed to apply a number of psychological tests and set up the War Office Selection Board system for identifying recruits with officer potential. The Air Force had always been considered a little less hidebound in creating its officer corps than the Army or the Navy; but by 1942 all three services were obliged to re-examine selection procedures. At Sir Stafford Cripps's suggestion the War Cabinet approved his proposal to set up a special Cabinet committee to enquire into the better use of psychologists and psychiatrists in the armed services, and the First Civil Service Commissioner was inspired to plan for the introduction of War Office selection methods into the first post-war competitions for admission into the Administrative Class.

As the war progressed, it became clear that the technologies being developed entailed modifications in the kind of leadership required on the battlefield. For example, tank battles were rarely tank versus tank combat, and were much more likely to be a form of assault with supporting infantry. As tanks became more vulnerable to infantry weapons, the proportion of infantry to tanks was increased within tank formations. At the beginning of the war there were six tank regiments to a single infantry battalion within an armoured division; at the end, four tank to five infantry battalions. Bernard Montgomery, in command on the 8th Army in the western desert, was a general with a flair for managing this mixture of tanks and infantry. He gained such a wide reputation for direct contract with his troops and the unorthodoxy of his field uniform that he became at times a fairly autonomous authority.

Ministers occasionally speculated about the effects of experience in the field on the political aspirations of the average conscript. They agreed that provisions for education classes at the battlefront were important in keeping up morale, and the Army Education Corps was expanded. The only subject of dispute was the Army Bureau of Current Affairs founded in August 1941 under W. E. Williams who had worked for Penguin Books. Some officials argued that the bureau was a major force in promoting left-wing opinions.

But the main thrust of ministerial activity in handling the political aspects of conscription was to face the problem of demobilization. The management of the economy raised the level of employment to unprecedented heights by the standards that had prevailed between the wars. There was a strong determination to avoid the economic slump of the early 1920s. Officials in tendering advice to Ministers were anxious to avoid what seemed to have been the mistakes made in the First World War. The government had then been compelled by mutinies to introduce a 'first in, first out' principle, after the War Office had unsuccessfully tried to release men according to the skills required by industry. Labour Ministers in the coalition were particularly sensitive to the response of the working classes to the experience of military service. But Conservatives were also concerned. Halifax had written to Duff Cooper in July 1940: 'I am quite certain that the human conscience in this country is not going to stand for a system that permits large numbers of unemployed'. Bevin when he reviewed the troops waiting to launch the invasion of Europe on the Normandy beaches had the advantage of knowing that the coalition was already committed to guarantee a high level of employment.

For three years, between the announcement of the conscription of women in December 1941 and the presentation in September and November 1944 of the coalition's final plans for releasing both members of the armed forces and production workers in the factories, different groups of officials had worked on demobilization plans. In 1942 the Reconstruction Secretariat gave high priority to considering alternative methods of releasing conscripts. It was then obvious that as soon as peace in Europe was declared the government would be expected to release several hundred thousand each month from the armed forces, and that manufacturing industry would have to redeploy some two million production workers. In 1942-3 the Ministry of Labour established its own enquiry into the tasks ahead; the Civil Service Commissioners took steps to make sure that the public services were in a good position to compete for available talent; and even the Colonial Office looked for soldiers with the right temperament for district administration. There were a number of enquiries into the opportunities which returning ex-servicemen should be offered, particularly in higher education and skilled crafts.

The final plans were designed to avoid the chaos of 1919. Only a few categories of workers, such as builders, were able to be released from the armed forces immediately for reconstruction work. The great majority were presented with their position in the demobilization order according to a scale based on age and length of service. Each 'demobbed' serviceman was to be given eight weeks' paid leave and 'resettlement advice'. Since 1943 married women had been drafted and they were given priority in the release of production workers.

The planning of demobilization had given scope for precisely that set of techniques in empirical observation which had enriched strategic planning. The social survey methods developed by the Ministry of Information in 1941-2 had much in common with operational research. Indeed, the transformation of that department in confidence and expertise was in itself concrete evidence of the coalition's handling of civilian morale. In March 1942 Bracken as the Minister of Information protested against the Cabinet's decision to introduce a censorship of opinion after Australian journalists in Britain had sent home articles criticizing the government's handling of the war in the Far East. His officials studiously kept to the principle that they should censor news stories on security grounds only, regardless of the Cabinet directive. By that date the department's own Social Survey team were conducting regular interviews to test opinion on the basis of sampling techniques. By contrast the Germans were testing public opinion through local officials of the Nazi Party whose estimates of morale had weaknesses comparable to those used in the Ministry of Information before the summer of 1941.[29] When the 'manpower survey' was developed to 'shake out' labour in all occupations, the Government Social Survey was on hand to devise ways of testing the consequences.

Chapter four
Economy and production

The mobilization of the economy for war production—the massive task of shifting resources from civilian to military uses—was not undertaken with a distinctive leadership comparable to Churchill's position in strategic affairs. The arrangements which the coalition government inherited from its predecessor were too complex and intractable to be drawn together into a single system. Hitler's attack on Russia in June 1941 had the effect not only of drawing attention to Soviet shortages of materials which Britain could supply but also of providing an example of Soviet central planning which some thought Britain should emulate. The model of Soviet war production was held up as an ideal to be copied in many circles during 1941-2 when Britain did not seem able to produce sufficient war material on time. But the system of administration devised to control both raw materials and government contracts owed far more to the invention of the generalist civil servant or the businessman recruited for special purposes than to any application of an overall plan. War production depended on the networks of commerce itself. Each industry which before the war had its own trade and research associations came to enjoy during the war a privileged relationship with the government agencies which were directed to sponsor its needs.

As the 'year alone' in 1940-41 had helped to clarify the discussion of strategic priorities, the first year of fighting in alliance with the United States and Russia in 1941-2 began to impose a new discipline on the organization of production and supply. The coalition government seemed at first to rely too much upon appealing to the 'Dunkirk spirit' of national unity which had been felt during 1940. In July that year the Ministry of Aircraft Production had asked people to turn out their old pots and pans to be collected as scrap metal which would compensate for a shortage of aluminium; appeals for other sources of metal, such as iron railings, followed this gesture. But during 1941 a body of opinion developed in Parliament and the country at large which laid the blame for poor results on failures in organization. The government departments responsible for supply were accused of incompetence by the Select Committee on National Expenditure. The 'production crisis' of 1942 and the decision to mobilize an even higher proportion of the country's manpower for the armed services coincided with the military disasters of the loss of the Far East and the retreat in the western desert.

But the 'production crisis' itself was resolved not so much by reforming the machinery of government as by relying on the American economy to carry the burden of supply. Churchill for along time resisted parliamentary pressure upon him to appoint a Minister of Production. When he did, the new Ministry which was already being described as a 'foreign office of supply' was soon regarded as the 'London end' of the United States War Production Board. Churchill refused to grasp the nettle of challenging Bevin's position at the Ministry of Labour as the supreme controller of manpower allocation. During 1942 most of the principal problems of war production were shifted from London-based Commonwealth consultations to the Washington-based system of combined boards. Jay Llewellin, who had served as parliamentary secretary in both the Ministry of Supply and that of Aircraft Production, as well as being the Minister himself at the latter for nine months, was sent to Washington as the resident minister for Supply. This appointment, announced in November 1942 and implemented in January 1943, symbolized the predominance of American resources.

The composition of the War Cabinet reflected Churchill's reluctance to place the control of manpower and the co-ordination of the supply departments in the same hands. There were three supply departments[1]—the Ministry of Supply itself created in 1939 to handle the needs of the War Office, the Ministry of Aircraft Production (created by Churchill in August 1940 for his friend, Beaverbrook, in order to take responsibility from the Air Ministry), and the Admiralty which was the only service department to retain direct control over its own material requirements. None of the men holding these three offices at different stages of the war was ever invited to join the War Cabinet, except Beaverbrook. He remained in the War Cabinet until February 1942 in four successive offices—Aircraft Production, Minister of State, Supply, and Production. Nor was the Minister of Food—a key office in supplying civilian needs—ever invited to join. Woolton who served in that office from the beginning of the coalition only entered the War Cabinet on becoming Minister of Reconstruction in November 1943.

The principal Ministers in the War Cabinet for the control of the economy were Bevin as Minister of Labour and Anderson as Lord President. The latter joined the War Cabinet in October 1940 on Chamberlain's resignation. During the course of 1941 the Lord

President's Committee over which Anderson presided came to take the leading position in dealing with all questions of wages, prices and home consumption. This committee also in 1941 took over the functions of the food policy committee which was designed to arbitrate between the Ministries of Agriculture and Food. Indeed by the beginning of 1942 this committee constituted almost a 'Home' Cabinet. By late 1942 five members of the War Cabinet (Bevin, Lyttelton, Attlee, Anderson and Morrison) were also members of the Lord President's Committee, the other three being Duncan (the Minister of Supply), Wood (The Chancellor of the Exchequer), and Cranborne (Lord Privy Seal and Leader of the House of Lords). After the reshuffle of February 1942 until november 1943 when Anderson himself replaced Wood as Chancellor, the Treasury had no higher ministerial representation that the Lord President's Committee which supervised the Home Guard and Fire Brigade were both attached to the Lord President's organization. The War Cabinet decided in 1942 that 'home front' ministers who were not a regular part of this apparatus should have their own private briefing meetings on an informal basis.

The Secretariats of the Committees surrounding the Lord President constituted the principal advisory staff on the 'home front'. At the end of 1940 the economists who had been recruited within the framework of the Cabinet Office, first to the survey of the war economy managed by Lord Stamp and then to what was called the Central Economic Information Service, were placed at the disposal of the Lord President's Committee. These economists became 'the Economic Section' of the Cabinet Office.

But there was no 'home front' equivalent of the fruitful relationships between scientists and serving officers in the field which played such an important part in managing the changing technology of war. Economists and administrators did not educate each other with the same élan as scientists and intelligence officers. The regional organization of the three supply ministries which came to be part of the Ministry of Production organization was in no way an effective 'field' listening service reporting back to headquarters, as the armed forces radio interception of enemy messages was able to do. Indeed, Lionel Robbins who became head of the 'Economic Section' has gone on record saying that the economists owed their success in wartime 'partly to our willingness to become part of the machine and to accept its logic rather pretend to some special status, and partly to the willingness with which the best elements among the Civil Service were prepared to co-operate'.[2] This co-operation was a much smaller and more highly centralized affair than the partnerships achieved in intelligence and strategic planning.

Nevertheless the arrangements for managing the 'home front' had a special impact on the political experience of the nation. First and foremost, the central administration began to learn the benefits of developing techniques of aggregation—how to calculate the gross domestic product and how to use such calculations in the apportionment of resources. Between the makeshift budgets of July and September 1940 and the first real budget of the coalition in April 1941, the economists in government drew upon advisers from outside, and the Treasury for the first time published statistical evidence in a White Paper in order to allay widespread fears of inflation. As the full implications of the American Congress's approval of lend-lease came to be understood during 1941-2, the central secretariats of the Lord President turned their attention to other problems of assessment and forecasting. Just as the combination of 'Ultra' intercepts and radar tracking had enabled Dowding to make the best use of all available fighter aircraft in 1940, the budgeting and forecasting methods devised in the Cabinet office in 1941-2 offered important opportunities for savings and the economic deployment of available men and materials.

The preparations made for the budget of April 1941 gave a great boost to the theories developed by J. M. Keynes who was himself brought into government after the creation of the coalition. In June 1940 he was appointed to the Chancellor of the Exchequer's advisory council and then given a roving commission on attachment to the Treasury. His diagnosis of the dangers of inflation in war finance was sufficiently convincing to persuade his colleagues that they should regard public finance as a crucial item within the larger whole of national income or output and the external balance of payments. Keynes was sure that the government could not rely on voluntary savings to draw off the excessive purchasing power for which consumer goods could not be provided, and he devised methods of compulsory saving which were in part accepted by the government. He also argued successfully against raising bank interest rates. The burden of post-war debt in 1945 which many anticipated after their experience of the 1920s was not wholly internally generated. The problems arose largely from the enforced sale of overseas investments.

Second, the Lord President's organization entailed a remarkable shift away from the rather narrow conception of the functions of government which before the war probably a majority of the officials had entertained. The same Treasury officials who had participated in the very cautious decisions taken on rearmament expenditure in the mid-1930s found themselves by 1943 with public disbursement of £11 million a day. This shift of view and circumstance was exemplified in the development of the notion of government departments as 'production authorities'. Government was no longer simply acting as the 'customer' of private firms and purchasing material for public use under contract, but was taking active steps to control the market itself. A department with 'production authority' functions played two roles. As the controller of the use of raw materials, it licensed each manufacturer to receive his allocation; as the sponsor of specific industrial interests, it sought from other departments the necessary authority for acquiring more labour or better capital investment. The Admiralty with its dockyards and the Ministry of Supply with its ordnance factories already enjoyed their own industrial establishments; other departments, such as the Board of Trade, could only become 'production authorities' by establishing direct contact with private firms. When the Ministry of Production in 1942 began preparing a guide to 'production authorities' for businessmen to use, it was assumed that all the major sectors of the economy had been covered. There was no area of economic activity which did not have some form of central 'sponsor'.

Theory and practice of production

Churchill could not impose on the apparatus of war production the same leadership which he applied to strategic command. He was not limited solely by his own predilections which were all in favour of managing the offensive, but was forcefully constrained by his own position as the leader of a coalition, and by the very structure of Cabinet government. The coalition emphasized rather than reduced the 'federal' nature of Cabinet relationships. Each of the ministers who came together in Cabinet had a set of departmental interests which might well conflict with that of his colleagues; each minister was technically the employer and manager of his staff. Even in war-time there was no way of avoiding the reconciliation of different departmental points of view through bargaining at Cabinet level. Nor was it easy to secure a form of arbitration which would decide between the conflicting claims of interested parties. Churchill's own position as Minister of Defence dominating the three ministers in charge of the service departments could not be reproduced in the domestic sphere without bringing forward a leader of almost comparable stature to the Prime Minister himself. Although from time to time Churchill toyed with the idea of making up a Cabinet of 'super ministers', each supervising a number of departmental ministers, he in fact remained largely committed to the principle that production departments should settle their differences and

effect their co-ordination through a process of bargaining between
their representatives.

Having set up Bevin as the symbol of trades union co-operation
in the war effort and as the supreme expression of the Labour
Party's commitment to a war against Fascism, Churchill could hardly
either reduce Bevin's status to that of a super minister's subordinate
or exaggerate the importance of the Ministry of Labour by bringing
all the supply departments under its aegis. The Prime Minister was
caught by his own sublety. His promotion of a trades union leader
from outside Parliament into the Cabinet to sit alongside the Labour
Party leaders, Attlee and Greenwood, limited his ability to promote
a form of 'home front' leadership from the Labour side of the coalition.
When Attlee and Greenwood did not show any marked success in
acting the roles of committee chairmen as independent arbitrators
above departmental interests, Churchill was inhibited in taking Bevin
further forward to even greater pre-eminence than that which the
latter had already achieved. The Secretary to the Cabinet in March
1941 told the Prime Minister that Attlee was incapable of dominating
powerful departments.[3] By that date Bevin had already been made
chairman of the Production Executive. The rationale of this body—as
Bevin explained to the House of Commons in January 1941—was
that 'the whole business of production and supply should be gripped
and controlled at the top by a small and compact directing body,
consisting of the ministers responsible for the executive departments
concerned.[4] Churchill at that stage dared not go faster than this
embodiment of Cabinet orthodoxy.

A theory of war production was developed in this context. Planning
was conceived as an activity which had to be undertaken simul-
taneously at the centre in the War Cabinet and in the individual
departments which sponsored particular industries. The differences
between centre and departments became almost a distinction between
programming and planning.[5] The centre had to relate the perceived
priorities of strategy to the known potential of industrial capacity
as expressed in men, machines and materials. The departments
were in the business of 'production planning', the allocation of man-
hours, plant capacity and raw materials to specific contracts or
particular firms. The centre tended to concentrate on the ends;
the departments on the means. But when departmental plans were
related to the programmes in the Cabinet arena where each
department had to justify its decisions, there was always a tendency
for central action to be built upon the reconciliation of departmental
claims to resources. The centre had to learn how to recognize
where departmental bids could be renegotiated, and departments
how to play for realistic needs. Far from overwhelming the con-

ventions of Cabinet government, the organization of war production seemed to caricature its bargaining procedures and to push its habits of bluffing and trading information down into industrial organization itself.

The advocacy of planning modelled on the experience of the Soviet Union, which naturally increased after the entry of Russia into the war in June 1941, was almost a moral reaction against the competitive systems which the coalition Cabinet had encouraged. The Soviets were thought by many critics of the government to be both simpler and more efficient in securing their production goals. The Association of Scientific Workers, for example, the British trades union with left-wing tendencies which was able to extend its membership as the skills it represented were more in demand, made regular references in its journal to the simplicity and directness of Soviet methods. The British system of war production seemed to combine what they regarded as the worst features of capitalist free enterprise and Cabinet government compromise. But those who praised the Soviet system were frequently at a loss to make specific recommendations. The closest approximation to a wholesale reform of the high command were the proposals made by Sir Stafford Cripps in the summer of 1942 when his advocacy of greater help for Russia caught the mood of popular concern about the management of the war effort. But his solutions were much more in keeping with British constitutional conventions than with Soviet planning. Cripps's ideas centred on a select committee system to monitor the executive function by function, and on a Cabinet of 'super ministers' untrammelled by departmental responsibility.[6] When the popular mood changed after the victories in the western desert, Churchill found it easy to ridicule such notions and to proceed with the plans he had already accepted for a Ministry of Production.[7]

Churchill's distinctive contribution to production planning was to improvise on Cabinet conventions by devising a War Cabinet committee, Defence Committee (Supply), over which he himself presided. It was a deliberate parallel to Defence Committee (Operations). What was unique to Defence Committee (Supply) was its composition of officials—a non-ministerial committee chaired by the Prime Minister which brought together staff officers from the services and the controllers or directors-general of the production departments. Established in June 1940, it was an official committee carrying the Prime Minister's authority. Ministers were invited to attend according to the subject discussed.

The achievement of the Defence Committee (Supply) was in the first few months of the coalition to give the Prime Minister a means of calculating a programme of production by surveying all the most important industrial fields. Its meetings characteristically ended not with a committee conclusion but with a Prime Minister's directive. Churchill used this committee in order to express his own priorities in strategic planning. For example, in the autumn of 1941 he used it as the forum for implementing his decision to put greater reliance in RAF Bomber command. The committee discussed a two-year programme for building up a first-line strength of 4,000 heavy bombers. These meetings revealed not only the short-falls in British industrial capacity and the advantages of American supply, but also the value to the Prime Minister of expertise which was not dependent on the production departments themselves. The Prime Minister's own statistical office under Lord Cherwell was a major source of programme calculations channelled through this committee. Through this office Churchill was always in a position to query the figures presented to him. The directives he sent out carried the ring of his personal conviction but were not always effectively heeded. The device of an official committee with the Prime Minister in the chair did not sit very well with arrangements made at ministerial level, and was an expression of the Prime Minister's own determination to cut through the mass of regulations rather than a supreme authority to which all were subordinate.

The heart of the war production system lay in the controls exercised over industry at the departmental level, qualified as they were by the Minister of Labour's powers to direct the labour force. These controls were not of the coalition's making, but were directly derived from the plans made by the Committee of Imperial Defence to institute emergency regulations as soon as hostilities began. What the coalition contributed after May 1940 was largely in the sphere of manpower budgeting. The Minister of Labour was also the Minister of National Service in charge of conscripting men and women into the armed forces, and perhaps even more significantly from the point of view of operations of government, of deciding how to deploy the Civil Service. Throughout the war the Treasury had to surrender its traditional control over the basic regulation of governmental establishments to a national system run by the Ministry of Labour.

The lessons of mistakes in production control were already being applied before the coalition was formed; its existence only accelerated the process of administrative change. There was in fact little room for manoeuvre in the rearmament programme. Churchill's government brought a new inspiration rather than any radical transformation in weapons production. It was already clear by March 1940 that the system of licensing would have to be replaced by one of allocation. When Churchill came to power, the system of regulation was already being adapted to counteract a failure to secure proper priorities.

The application of emergency legislation by departments in fact led to the creation of special departments which, although given the usual ministerial form, were largely creatures of the control process alone. In only two cases were the new ministries attached to existing departments: just as the Minister of Labour was also Minister of National Service, so the Home Secretary was also Minister of Home Security.[8] The three 'supply departments' had to work with such new creations as the Ministry of Fuel and Power, the Ministry of Economic Warfare and the Ministry of War Transport. All three had taken functions from the Board of Trade, and were the products of defence regulation not parliamentary statute.

Fuel and Power, to which Gwilym Lloyd-George was appointed as Minister in June 1942, was the only department to have its origins in a coalition compromise. Economic Warfare, although important to many Labour MPs who were pleased to see it placed in the hands of a Labour Minister, Hugh Dalton, when the coalition was formed, had been planned by an official committee before the war; War Transport was an administrative amalgamation of Transport and Shipping in May 1941. But Fuel and Power was an extended version of the Mines Department of the Board of Trade after Labour ministers had decided that they could not endanger the government by pressing for the nationalization of the coal industry.[9]

The major contributions of coalition discussions to this apparatus of regulation was to place the Minister of Labour and National Service in an unique position *vis à vis* other departments. Ironically, Bevin had begun in this office hoping that he could proceed a long way in mobilizing the labour force without using any powers of compulsion. He thought most workers would respond to persuastion. If compulsion was to be used, he wanted to exploit it as a means of improving conditions of work. For example, in directing the dock labour force away from ports vulnerable to bombing he succeeded in introducing a scheme which removed casual labour arrangements, made the docker into permanent employees of the new regional port directors, and gave them a guaranteed minimum wage. But by the winter of 1940-41 it was clear that Bevin could no longer be sparing in the use of his powers. The great majority of the directions then issued were to draft men into building and civil engineering. They were rarely used for women.

Beveridge's report on manpower requirements in December 1940 demonstrated a conflict of priorities between the manpower needs of war production and those of the armed services. The only method of solving the problem required a rethinking of the deployment of skilled labour and a fresh approach to the conscription of women.

In January 1941, the Cabinet approved the strengthening of Bevin's powers in three directions. First, he was allowed to change the basis on which certain occupations were exempted from military service. In future the exemption was to be given to specific firms registered as 'protected establishments' and not to categories of worker. Second, he was authorized to register men and women falling outside the ages of military service so that they could be directed into essential work. This registration made it possible to make up for any short-fall in munitions labour by bringing more women into employment. Third, he was empowered to designate 'essential work' by order-in-council and thus hold staff in their jobs. Employers were not allowed to dismiss any worker in an 'essential' establishment without the permission of a Ministry of Labour official, the National Service Officer.

What these powers made possible was an assessment of the structure of the working population for a form of programming in manpower allocation to which all other departments in the administration had to submit, as soon as the Lord President's Committee had taken its decisions. Like the supply departments, the Ministry of Labour had a regional organization which held together hundreds of local labour exchange offices. An important new element was introduced in December 1941 when district manpower boards composed entirely of officials, who were often temporary civil servants specially recruited for the purpose, were established in forty-four major cities where the implementation of the Minister's decisions presented the greatest problems. These boards decided individual applications for deferment—exemption from or postponement of military service—and also examined the pattern of employment in their districts. They became an essential tool in achieving the maximum use of available manpower. By the summer of 1942 the Ministry of Labour was in a stronger position to compel other departments to face the incompatibilities of the armed forces and industry, each with conflicting requirements. But the turning point came in 1943 when the nation's resources were fully stretched in preparation for the invasion of Europe. The Ministry of Labour was no longer required to reconcile competing demands for manpower; the Cabinet had to determine what could be made available and then ask the Ministry to administer the allocations it had made. In December 1943 Churchill led the Cabinet in making the greatest cut-backs in the allocation to the armed forces rather than sacrificing the effort in weapons production or increasing the austerity of civilian standards of living.

The forms of production planning therefore depended on links between departments and firms, criss-crossed with Ministry of Labour designations of reserved occupations and essential work. It has been estimated that some 30,000 private firms were drawn into the production of war material. The supply departments issuing the contracts and other departments, such as the Board of Trade, which promoted specific industries, were forced to develop a network of sponsorship arrangements with varying degrees of intimacy. The relationship between the customer and the contractor depended on the size, organization and equipment of the material at the latter's disposal and also on technical requirements for assembling the finished product. The most intimate relationships, such as those between the Ministry of Aircraft Production and airframe manufacturers such as A. V. Roe, took their origins from the rearmament plans of the 1930s. At that time 'group organizations' were formed to link together a number of key firms. For example, in 1936 a scheme for the manufacture of Bristol aeroplane engines brought together five firms under the leadership of Austin Motors. But large firms would at the same time also complicate the methods of control by relying on sub-contracting to small firms which made individual pieces for subsequent assembly. BSA, the principle makers of the Browning machine gun, assembled the different components of this weapon from the parts delivered by its sub-contractors. The supply departments themselves often contracted with an individual supplier for particular components, such as a gun turret or an aeroplane undercarriage, which were then distributed as a 'free issue' to their principal manufacturing contractors. It was often difficult to distinguish between components ordered directly by government and components supplied under private arrangements between principal contractors and their sub-contractors.

Indeed, the basic distinction between private ventures and official sponsorship was continuously blurred. Each of the three supply departments developed its own set of principles for deciding how to allocate work between state factories and private firms. The Air Ministry and the Ministry of Aircraft Production were much more closely involved with a 'family' of nominally private contractors than were the Admiralty or Ministry of Supply. The majority of firms in the munitions business did not compete for orders, and had government guarantees against loss. The Air Ministry during the 1930s had cultivated sixteen aircraft and four engine firms, and hesitated to admit any outsiders into this circle. Sometimes the boundary between public firms and private firms was shifted to permit changes in the scope of production. The motor and locomotive firms which had originally been contracted to make tanks, such as Vauxhall in its manufacture of the Churchill tank, found towards the end of the war that the Ministry of Supply preferred to switch over to the Royal Ordnance Factories. The three oldest factories of this kind were organized to act as 'parents' to others. Work was also allotted to the hybrid enterprises—the agency factory, a set of buildings and plant machinery in public ownership which was then hired to a private management. The 'production authorities' both took work to labour by placing contracts where there was spare capacity and took work to buildings and management by commissioning unused facilities.

The practice of government sponsorship in industry was less authoritarian than the structure of departmental control implied, because the majority of private firms wanted to 'get in on the act'. They found that they could participate in war production without making any very fundamental changes in their location or organization. Indeed, when the Board of Trade tried to enforce 'concentration' on particular sectors of industry by using its powers of control over raw materials to establish a 'nucleus factory' which would release labour elsewhere for the war effort, it found that many of the enterprises it intended to transform had already secured 'essential work' from another departmental source. The mobilization of the labour force involved much less movement than the Minister of Labour's powers of direction suggested. British war production followed very closely all the imperfections of scale and dispersal associated with pre-war industry. Its dependence on small firms and inadequate machine tools was underlined as soon as the American economy swung into full gear. In assembling aircraft, for example, the average production per factory unit in the United States was sixty a week; the comparable figure for Britain was ten. Although the smaller scale and less specialized nature of British firms made it easier for them than for the United States equivalents to alter the design of standard weapons, they could never have produced sufficient material for a long war. The flexibility which enabled designers to attempt forty-one 'marks' of the Merlin engine and twenty 'marks' of the Spitfire aeroplane was as much a testimony to the conservatism of industrial organization as to the inventiveness of industrial entrepreneurship.

It was precisely the continuance of traditional methods by the system of departmental controls that aroused the greatest amount of public protest in 1941, as Rommel's armies continued to push back the British forces in North Africa. People in the factories who expected to see the results of their efforts through success in the battlefield were disenchanted and turned their attention to the shortcomings of the government's arrangements. Both workers and civil servants who lived close to the realities of administrative controls tended to emphasise their idiotic and inefficient aspects. The surveys of opinion conducted by Mass Observation in 1941-2 were used by several commentators to place a clear construction on popular perceptions of the production system.[10] It was argued that government had too 'economic' an approach to human incentives and was neglecting 'human relations'. The case was put against using methods of 'crude conscription and in favour of developing conscription by intelligence'—work suitable for individual temperament and training. In the anxieties of the moment, public attention was focused on deficiencies in the administrative machinery.

The civil service itself was particularly vulnerable to the depression in national morale, when a lot of popular criticism took the form of attacking 'red tape'. The trades unions in the public sector were in fact in the vanguard in exposing inefficiencies. The staff side of the National Whitley Council pointed out to the Treasury where the greatest scandals in the deployment of manpower could be exposed, and unnecessary work eliminated. The civil service unions in 1941 wanted the suspension of those sections of the Trades Disputes Act which prevented their affiliation to the TUC and which forbade local authorities to make union membership a condition of employment, because they felt they were being unfairly treated if they could not negotiate directly with management at the local level, as their private sector counterparts could do. The Treasury was slow to respond. It began by promoting better business methods, and by negotiating a new national agreement on conditions of work. A Treasury circular in May 1941 extended the normal working week of the Civil Service and curtailed the length of annual leave. But the unions gained no satisfaction over the Trades Disputes Act. Churchill resolutely refused to contemplate changes which he felt would antagonize the overwhelming majority of the Conservative Party. Labour ministers to the annoyance of the TUC were not able to persuade him to change his mind.

The greatest obstacle to any more extensive reform of working methods was the constitutional position of each minister as the employer and manager of his staff. The authority of the Treasury to interfere with the internal methods of each department was tempered by the special character of its minister's interests. It was characteristic of the Treasury's response to demands for a better approach to business management that the Organization and Methods division which it created in 1941 from a few inspectors of office machinery was not regarded as part of the central department proper, but treated as a 'common service' to departments which was conducted with the advice of an advisory panel of businessmen. The Treasury moved very cautiously in its approach to improving its methods of personnel management, and was the subject of a great deal of criticism in the House of Commons where several MPs supported the proposal that a separate 'civil service department' should be created to instil a proper sense of efficiency in other departments. Wilson Smith at the early age of 37 was appointed Treasury Establishments Officer in May 1942 to try to persuade departments that they should learn how to co-operate to improve efficiency and to prepare for reconstruction.

The manpower and production 'crises' of 1941-2 therefore exposed the weaknesses of interdepartmental relationships. Although the argument in Parliament and in the press was framed in terms of the need for administrative reform or for a 'supreme authority' in production matters, the debate was also to some degree a critique of the industrial system which traditionally divided the supporters of the two major parties. The critiques of Cabinet government were in fact oblique expressions of two totally different sets of hopes and expectations for the production system itself, and it seemed likely that these hopes would continue to point in opposing directions after the war. Conservatives feared that the system established the precedents of 'bureaucratic socialism'; Labour supporters that it gave ample scope for granting the privileges of 'corporate power' to capitalism. People of all shades of opinion had the feeling that the war had in some way already established a new social order by compelling experiments in government and social organization. One of the reasons why reconstruction questions were always being introduced during immediate crises of confidence was that each social class expected to enjoy the rewards of sacrifice with its own form of guaranteed compensation after the peace. The psychological effects of mass mobilization were to invest the debate on the organization of supreme command with the ideological overtones of class conflict. Whenever questions of reconstruction and civilian morale were intermixed with party beliefs, ministers tended to want private meetings in party groupings. Throughout the war both Conservative and Labour ministers met informally and separately to discuss common anxieties.

It was impossible to find a minister for a single departmental virtuoso performance that would stimulate production and improve morale, as Beaverbrook's appointment as Minister of Aircraft Production had done. Beaverbrook himself in October 1940 had declined Churchill's suggestion that he should combine that office with that of the second supply department and become jointly responsible for Aircraft and Supply. This task was beyond the energies even of Beaverbrook. But his performance in either Aircraft Production or Supply had hardly encouraged interdepartmental co-operation. Indeed, on the contrary, Beaverbrook had gone a long way towards antagonizing other ministries by securing his own priorities only by making piratical raids on other agencies or by refusing to allow his officials to join in negotiations. He was always likely to provoke a clash with Bevin; as he admitted, he was an individualist and an improviser, not a committee man. As the proprietor of the *Daily Express,* he gave his disputes with Bevin something of the character of an *Express* campaign against the *Daily Herald.* It was 'the Beaver's' maverick and clubbable qualities that endeared him to the Prime Minister who on a number of occasions toyed with the idea of making him into a 'production supremo'.

Churchill clung as long as he could to the notion that the best method of securing a national production programme was to rely on the reconciliation of different departmental interests through the representatives of those interests themselves. It was said that Chamberlain in the early months of 1940 might have sanctioned the appointment of a Minister of Production. Churchill waited until February 1942 before committing himself to this decision.

His first action on taking office in May 1940 had been to set up the Production Council, a ministerial committee consisting of the supply ministers, the President of the Board of Trade, and the Minister of Labour, but under the independent chairmanship of the Minister without portfolio, Arthur Greenwood. The Council's industrial capacity committee made the first moves in reforming the regional organization of the supply departments in the country at large; its principal priority officers' committee instigated methods for deciding which weapons were to be given priority. The Council worked through the Central Priority Department of the Ministry of Supply. After many criticisms had been voiced about the anomaly of the Ministry of Supply's position, Churchill in his reconsideration of the structure of Cabinet Committees in January 1941 plumped for a Production Executive to parallel an Import Executive. Both bodies included the supply ministers, but on the first they were joined by the Minister of Labour and on the second by the President of the Board of Trade and the Minister of Food. Neither body had an independent chairman. In Parliament Churchill defended the idea that the only way to coherent action was to get the ministers responsible to come to a decision by joint agreement.

Bevin as Minister of Labour was the chairman of the Production Executive. Its system of committees and secretariat constituted the heart of the war production system in 1941. But it gained the reputation for being as much a battleground between ministers as a place for decision, partly because Beaverbrook as the Minister of Supply was reluctant to surrender what he saw as his final responsibility for the allocation of raw materials. Its most important contribution to the war effort was to improve the system of area boards—twelve in number for the whole country—where district officials from the supply departments received the advice of local industrialists and trades unionists. It was at this level that the frustrations of the production system were most apparent. In the summer of 1941 these area boards were given a new list of duties and empowered to set up capacity clearing centres—an important step forward in identifying spare industrial capacity.

Churchill only acted to change the structure again after the United States had entered the war. He thought that the British government should be in a position to treat directly on an equal footing with Donald Nelson, the newly appointed chairman of the American War Production Board. This opportunity enabled the Prime Minister to bring together two different proposals from the many with which he had been bombarded—the idea of appointing a 'super minister' to direct the supply departments and the suggestion that there should be a production general staff which serviced the production authority in a similar manner to the Chiefs of Staff giving advice to the War Cabinet. Rapidly but carefully a definition of the office of Minister of Production was devised. Beaverbrook, Churchill's first choice for the post, lasted in the office only fourteen days (10-24 February 1942) after a 'nervous breakdown', which arose partly from his failure to win agreement to his securing control over manpower, and partly from his anticipation that the Prime Minister would fall from power. He was succeeded by Oliver Lyttelton who stayed for the remainder of the war.

The post of the Minister of Production carried membership of the War Cabinet, but his functions were defined in negative terms. The new Minister could not overrule the existing supply ministers who retained a right of appeal to the Minister of Defence. He was allowed only to give general directions, supervision and guidance. Lyttelton grasped with enthusiasm the proposal for a production general staff. For the duration of the war the Joint War Production Staff advising the Minister became the principal link between the production planning system of the United States and the British supply departments. In addition, the area boards supervised by the Production Executive came under the chairmanship of controllers appointed by the new Ministry. Although the new Minister lacked the full executive powers of his fellow members of Cabinet, he headed both a central planning and a regional organization. This was a subtle variation on traditional constitutional themes which would hardly have succeeded but for the inauguration of combined boards to unite American and British efforts.

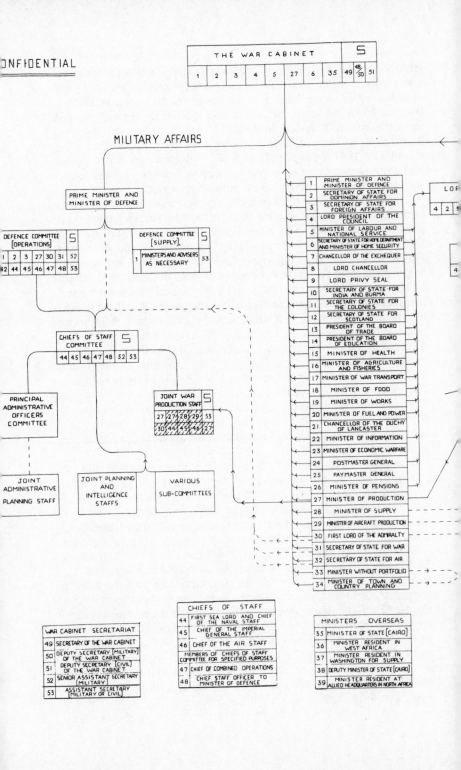

CONFIDENTIAL

THE WAR CABINET		5		
1	2	3	4	5	27	6	35	49	48/50	51

MILITARY AFFAIRS

PRIME MINISTER AND MINISTER OF DEFENCE

DEFENCE COMMITTEE [OPERATIONS]	5
1	2	3	27	30	31	52
32	44	45	46	47	48	53

DEFENCE COMMITTEE [SUPPLY]	5
MINISTERS AND ADVISERS AS NECESSARY	1 ... 53

CHIEFS OF STAFF COMMITTEE	5
44	45	46	47	48	52	53

PRINCIPAL ADMINISTRATIVE OFFICERS COMMITTEE

JOINT WAR PRODUCTION STAFF	5
27	27	28	29	53
30	44	45	46	27

JOINT ADMINISTRATIVE PLANNING STAFF

JOINT PLANNING AND INTELLIGENCE STAFFS

VARIOUS SUB-COMMITTEES

1	PRIME MINISTER AND MINISTER OF DEFENCE
2	SECRETARY OF STATE FOR DOMINION AFFAIRS
3	SECRETARY OF STATE FOR FOREIGN AFFAIRS
4	LORD PRESIDENT OF THE COUNCIL
5	MINISTER OF LABOUR AND NATIONAL SERVICE
6	SECRETARY OF STATE FOR HOME DEPARTMENT AND MINISTER OF HOME SECURITY
7	CHANCELLOR OF THE EXCHEQUER
8	LORD CHANCELLOR
9	LORD PRIVY SEAL
10	SECRETARY OF STATE FOR INDIA AND BURMA
11	SECRETARY OF STATE FOR THE COLONIES
12	SECRETARY OF STATE FOR SCOTLAND
13	PRESIDENT OF THE BOARD OF TRADE
14	PRESIDENT OF THE BOARD OF EDUCATION
15	MINISTER OF HEALTH
16	MINISTER OF AGRICULTURE AND FISHERIES
17	MINISTER OF WAR TRANSPORT
18	MINISTER OF FOOD
19	MINISTER OF WORKS
20	MINISTER OF FUEL AND POWER
21	CHANCELLOR OF THE DUCHY OF LANCASTER
22	MINISTER OF INFORMATION
23	MINISTER OF ECONOMIC WARFARE
24	POSTMASTER GENERAL
25	PAYMASTER GENERAL
26	MINISTER OF PENSIONS
27	MINISTER OF PRODUCTION
28	MINISTER OF SUPPLY
29	MINISTER OF AIRCRAFT PRODUCTION
30	FIRST LORD OF THE ADMIRALTY
31	SECRETARY OF STATE FOR WAR
32	SECRETARY OF STATE FOR AIR
33	MINISTER WITHOUT PORTFOLIO
34	MINISTER OF TOWN AND COUNTRY PLANNING

LOR...
| 4 | 2 | |

WAR CABINET SECRETARIAT	
49	SECRETARY OF THE WAR CABINET
50	DEPUTY SECRETARY [MILITARY] OF THE WAR CABINET
51	DEPUTY SECRETARY [CIVIL] OF THE WAR CABINET
52	SENIOR ASSISTANT SECRETARY [MILITARY]
53	ASSISTANT SECRETARY [MILITARY OR CIVIL]

CHIEFS OF STAFF	
44	FIRST SEA LORD AND CHIEF OF THE NAVAL STAFF
45	CHIEF OF THE IMPERIAL GENERAL STAFF
46	CHIEF OF THE AIR STAFF
47	MEMBERS OF CHIEFS OF STAFF COMMITTEE FOR SPECIFIED PURPOSES
47	CHIEF OF COMBINED OPERATIONS
48	CHIEF STAFF OFFICER TO MINISTER OF DEFENCE

MINISTERS OVERSEAS	
35	MINISTER OF STATE [CAIRO]
36	MINISTER RESIDENT IN WEST AFRICA
37	MINISTER RESIDENT IN WASHINGTON FOR SUPPLY
38	DEPUTY MINISTER OF STATE [CAIRO]
39	MINISTER RESIDENT AT ALLIED HEADQUARTERS IN NORTH AFRICA

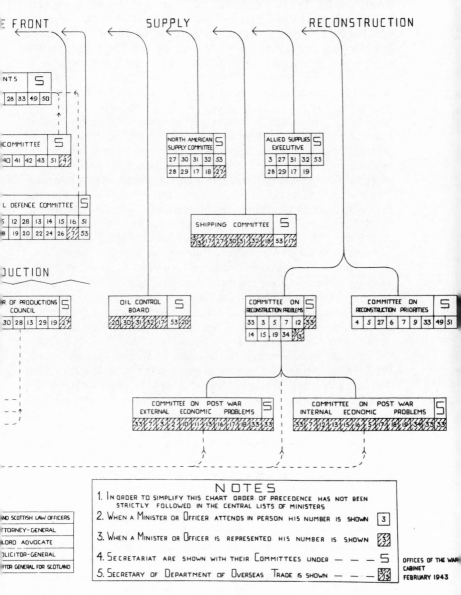

THE
CENTRAL EXECUTIVE GOVERNMENT
OF
GREAT   BRITAIN

E FRONT   SUPPLY   RECONSTRUCTION

NTS ⊑
28 33 49 50

COMMITTEE ⊑
40 41 42 43 51

L DEFENCE COMMITTEE ⊑
5 12 28 13 14 15 16 51
8 19 20 22 24 26 53

UCTION

R OF PRODUCTIONS COUNCIL ⊑
30 28 13 29 19

NORTH AMERICAN SUPPLY COMMITTEE ⊑
27 30 31 32 53
28 29 17 18

ALLIED SUPPLIES EXECUTIVE ⊑
3 27 31 32 53
28 29 17 19

SHIPPING COMMITTEE ⊑
13 17 27 30 31 32 18 53

OIL CONTROL BOARD ⊑
30 30 31 32 53 20

COMMITTEE ON RECONSTRUCTION PROBLEMS ⊑
33 3 5 7 12 33
14 15 19 34

COMMITTEE ON RECONSTRUCTION PRIORITIES ⊑
4 5 27 6 7 9 33 49 51

COMMITTEE ON POST WAR EXTERNAL ECONOMIC PROBLEMS ⊑
33 3 2 10 11 12 16 17 18 33 53

COMMITTEE ON POST WAR INTERNAL ECONOMIC PROBLEMS ⊑
33 12 13 15 16 17 18 19 34 53

ND SCOTTISH LAW OFFICERS
TTORNEY-GENERAL
LORD ADVOCATE
OLICITOR-GENERAL
ITOR GENERAL FOR SCOTLAND

N O T E S
1. IN ORDER TO SIMPLIFY THIS CHART ORDER OF PRECEDENCE HAS NOT BEEN
   STRICTLY FOLLOWED IN THE CENTRAL LISTS OF MINISTERS
2. WHEN A MINISTER OR OFFICER ATTENDS IN PERSON HIS NUMBER IS SHOWN   3
3. WHEN A MINISTER OR OFFICER IS REPRESENTED HIS NUMBER IS SHOWN   ▨
4. SECRETARIAT ARE SHOWN WITH THEIR COMMITTEES UNDER — — — ⊑
5. SECRETARY OF DEPARTMENT OF OVERSEAS TRADE IS SHOWN — — — ▨

OFFICES OF THE WAR
CABINET
FEBRUARY 1943

Aggregation at the centre

The principal organizational feature of the coalition on the 'home
front' was the co-ordinating committee of ministers and/or officials
strongly supported by a specialist secretariat. When the Americans
in 1942 asked their British allies for a guide to the 'central executive'
which would give in a diagrammatic form the membership of the
inter-locking committees, John Martin, one of Churchill's private
secretaries, produced a chart which marked each secretariat with
a capital S (see Diagram pp. 98-9). This diagram which was regularly
revised has subsequently become an essential tool for the beginner
who wishes to explore the coalition. By 1942-3 there were four main
main areas of committee/secretariat activity—the home front in
general, production, supply and reconstruction—each concerned
with various methods for aggregating data about the economy and
the war effort. The secretariats in production and supply were by
that date closely tied into the Anglo-American system of joint planning.
The improvisations in Cabinet organizations of 1940-41 became the
major British contribution to the creation of Anglo-American combined boards in 1942-3. After the winter of 1942-3 the presence of
American institutions and personnel at the heart of British government
restricted the scope for fundamental organizational change.

The cautious approach taken by Churchill to establishing the
Ministry of Production seemed to exemplify the faith which had by
that time been placed in the formula of a co-ordinating committee
with a secretariat. An essential part of the Ministry of Production
was the Minister's Council, a co-ordinating committee consisting
of the supply ministers, with the President of the Board of Trade,
the Minister of Labour and the Minister of Works—almost the old
Production Executive in a new guise. While the production crisis
was being debated, Churchill had also resisted pressure upon him
from ministers and officials in favour of establishing a new 'Ministry
of Planning'. Reith, who had been made Minister of Works and
Buildings in October 1940, wished to see the responsibility for physical
planning firmly established within his own department which had a
direct interest in planned rebuilding after bomb damage. He
established a committee to examine the compensation and betterment
questions to legislate to set up a 'central planning authority'.[11] Churchill
attached the title 'planning' to the department's title when he
appointed Reith's successor, Lord Portal, in the February 1942
reshuffle, but did nothing to satisfy the department's claim that it
should be given the complete supervision of physical
reconstruction.

The model for reconciling different departmental interests was
the Lord President's Committee to which the Economic Section of

the Cabinet Office was attached as part of its secretariat. This committee was originally envisaged as a means of co-ordinating the economic committees of Cabinet, having a general watching brief over economic development as well as dealing with any special questions which arose from time to time, such as the accommodation to be provided for government departments. But after the reshuffle of Cabinet committees in January 1941 and the debate on production it gradually superseded a number of lesser committees and became by the beginning of 1942 a 'home front' Cabinet. Its relationship with the Production Executive and the Ministry of Production was never clearly defined, but the boundary between Lord President's work and production work was usually drawn where the effects of shifting more resources from civilian consumption had to be handled separately from the allocation of resources themselves. The Lord President presided over the maintenance of civilian morale, and his committee handled all the tricky domestic questions such as coal rationing, demobilization and education reform. With the American entry into the war and the dropping of all pretences that British war production was a self-sufficient system, the Lord President's Committee acquired its supreme importance by handling the allocation of manpower. Its secretariat learnt how to aggregate the relevant data by constructing a 'manpower budget'—a tally of all sectors of employment could be used to identify where cuts and transfers should be made.

Anderson, who remained Lord President from October 1940 until he was replaced by Attlee in September 1943, took with him the responsibility for manpower calculations when he became Chancellor of the Exchequer. He also retained the chairmanship of the Machinery of Government Committee which had previously been attached to the Lord President's office. In his three years as Lord President Anderson enjoyed Churchill's complete confidence. He and Sir James Grigg were the two former administrators turned ministers in whom the Prime Minister placed great faith. When there were strong differences between ministers on the implications of the Beveridge report, Churchill entrusted Anderson with the chairmanship of the newly formed Reconstruction Priorities Committee which was intended to sort out the difficulties. Anderson also had charge of the highly secret administrative arrangements for the construction of the first atomic bomb, and presided over the Tube Alloys Consultative Council, the cover name of the atomic energy project's major authority.

When Sir Kingsley Wood died in September 1943 Churchill hesitated over finding a successor as Chancellor of the Exchequer. He decided to send Anderson to the Treasury only after three days of delay and deliberation. There seemed to be a number of candidates with equal claims, including the Minister of Production, Lyttelton. Churchill also used the opportunity of a small reshuffle to bring Beaverbrook back into the government, this time as Lord Privy Seal but without a seat in the War Cabinet.

But the Economic Section of the Cabinet Office did not follow Anderson to the Treasury. Its independence of the Treasury as a committee secretariat was the key to its influence and success. By the time of Kingsley Wood's death it had established a form of providing regular advice to the Lord President's Committee on the performance of the war economy which was vital to that committee's decisions about the proportion of national resources to be diverted from civilian to military purposes. The Economic Section, like its fellow unit created from the Central Economic Information Service at the end of 1940, the Central Statistical Office, acquired a reputation for pressing the case in favour of imposing extreme austerity on civilian life, the minimum provisions of personal consumption necessary for health and morale.[12] The Central Statistical Office, unlike the Economic Section, was not attached to the Lord President's Committee; but instead it provided the War Cabinet as a whole with regular digests of information. What gave the Economic Section its greatest influence after 1942 was its participation in the secretariat of two important Cabinet committees, the Manpower Committee and the Shipping Committee. Those who constructed both 'manpower budgets' and 'shipping budgets' had the benefits of specialist economic advice.

Co-operation between economists of different views had the value in developing economic theory through direct application. Government service came closer to the ideals of intellectual debate than the universities themselves. Lionel Robbins has recorded how Keynes and Robertson awakened him during the war from 'dogmatic slumbers'.[13] The displacement of the Treasury from the centre of economic affairs made it easier to put together and consider the two complementary sides of Keynesian theory—the macroeconomic problems of controlling levels of expenditure and the microeconomic mechanics of allocating resources between different investments.

The civil affairs side of the Cabinet Secretariat (servicing the Lord President's Committee, its sub-committees and its association with production, supply, and reconstruction committees) was the administrative heart of the coalition, but one in which the Prime Minister himself did not participate directly. The military affairs side in John Martin's diagram of the central executive is where the Prime Minister himself appears in person. Churchill was dependent for his knowledge of civil affairs particularly on routine meetings with Bridges, the Cabinet Secretary, and with Norman Brook who from March 1942 to November 1943 was deputy secretary on the civil side. Insofar as Ismay had a civilian parallel in the confidence of the Prime Minister, Brook played that role.

The growth of the civil affairs side of the Cabinet Office displaced the Treasury from its central position in domestic policy. This eclipse was also partly due to the lack of sympathy between the Prime Minister and the permanent secretary of the Treasury, Sir Horace Wilson, who had been Neville Chamberlain's principal adviser until the coalition was formed. The Chancellor of the Exchequer, Sir Kingsley Wood, had a special relationship with Churchill in Conservative Party affairs, but that did not mean that the Treasury as a department was able to extend its influence under its minister's personal access to the Prime Minister. The power of the Minister of Labour also limited the Treasury's status in Whitehall. Wood was asked to surrender his seat in the War Cabinet to facilitate the reshuffle of February 1942. The management of the war effort after the American government had passed the Lend-Lease Act in March 1941 transformed the work of the overseas finance division which had previously paid for goods from the United States by the sale of foreign securities. American credit facilities required a permanent Treasury delegation in Washington.

The shift towards United States organizations of the whole civil affairs and production apparatus, as in military affairs, took place during the course of 1942. The system of combined boards was inaugurated in January, and the Combined Production and Resources Board which was designed to give effect to the supply side of an agreed order of battle first met in June when the new British Minister of Production visited Washington. The meshing of American and British arrangements required both a revision of standardization which could marry the products of different assembly lines. The Americans wanted to introduce priority ratings which measured British requests in terms of American equivalents of strategic value; the American 'standard products committee' wanted to programme as accurately as possible all foreseeable calls on the Unites States' industrial capacity for the next two years. The British Embassy in Washington was already at the centre of a number of departmental missions, and the idea of appointing a 'co-ordinating minister' had frequently been suggested. By the time Llewellin arrived in January 1943 to take up the new post of Minister Resident in Washington, the British authorities acknowledged that it would be more convenient to centre supply questions in Washington rather than in London. The British Supply Council under the new minister co-ordinated British participation in the combined boards, and its London counterpart, the North American Supply Committee, was completely overshadowed by its own secretariat. The classic combination of Committee plus secretariat became almost entirely an official apparatus working with the Ministry of Production.

The assessments made in the light of Anglo-American Joint Planning concentrated Cabinet attention on the major problem of re-allocating manpower during 1943. The new Joint War Production Staff of the Minister of Production saw that it had to relate the demands of the services for manpower to meet figures agreed with the Americans, and the demands of the production programmes for skilled labour on munitions. During the summer of 1942 the civil affairs secretariat turned its attention from the relatively minor task of trying to 'shake out' from the Civil Service more manpower for the armed services to the major business of drawing up the first attempt at a full manpower budget. In March 1942 the British Chiefs of Staff had agreed that by April 1943 Britain would equip 25 armoured divisions and 125 infantry divisions.

From this point of central secretariat work onwards, it was assumed that 1943 would witness the fullest extent of commitment to industrial production and 1944 a definite switch to the fullest mobilization of the armed forces for the proposed invasion of Europe. As the concept of a two-stage ending to the war was developed—first victory in Europe and then victory against Japan—all plans for war industry rested on the assumption that there would be three stages: Stage I began with the Allied invasion of Europe, Stage II with the German submission, and Stage III with the Japanese submission. In spite of some hesitation in the autumn of 1944 when the War Cabinet thought that the war with Germany would be finished by the end of the year, the manpower allocations of 1944 continued to be made on the assumption that victory would have been achieved in Europe by 30 June 1945. Even this seemed optimistic after the German counter-attack in the Ardennes, and between January and March 1945 there were still provisional plans that the war production system would have to continue until November. It was only in the second week of April that the end of hostilities in Europe came to be expected by 31 May.

The most critical period in the working out of these planning assumptions was between America's entry into the war and the German Navy's withdrawal of its U-boats from the Atlantic in May 1943. The weakest link in the Anglo-American war production system was the transport of material by sea across the Atlantic. Unknown to the Allies, German intelligence had broken the code used to give instructions to convoys of shipping, and Admiral Doenitz was therefore in a good position to use his submarines to their greatest effect. British cryptographers on the other hand were placed in total darkness by the introduction of the Triton code for German submarines in February 1942. Before that date, and particularly after the capture of U-boat 110 in May 1941, Britain had been able to intercept German naval messages. It was not until December 1942 that the Triton code was broken, or until April—May 1943 that the Admiralty submarine tracking room was able once again to use all sources of intelligence to direct the Allies against the U-boats. During 1942 over 6 million tons of Allied shipping in all waters had been torpedoed by German submarines, and in March 1943 the monthly figures of tonnage lost were close to the worst losses of November 1942. Allied convoys were issued with a new code in June 1943, in case the Germans had broken the old one, and what had become known as 'the Battle of the Atlantic' was by the Autumn of 1943 reduced to a less disastrous level of combat.

Churchill's response to the crisis was to place himself in the chair of a special Cabinet committee, the Anti-U Boat Warfare Committee set up in November 1942 to create a suitably high-powered forum in which to debate the issues and decide the action. But from the point of view of an improved Cabinet secretariat, the necessary action had already been taken with the appointment of the Shipping Committee in May 1942. With the creation of the Ministry of Production, the Import Executive, which had paralleled the Production Executive, was wound up and its place taken by the Shipping Committee under Harcourt Johnston, the secretary of the Department of Overseas Trade, a junior minister. The composition of this committee was otherwise entirely official, with a secretariat joining the Cabinet Office and the Ministry of War Transport, bringing together representatives from the services, production departments, food distribution and transport.

The shipping Committee was a symbol both of the massive contribution made to the war effort by an accurate aggregation of data, and of the supreme importance of Anglo-American co-operation. By the end of the war the Allies controlled the greater part of the world's shipping. Ironically in view of the great sacrifices made in the Battle of the Atlantic, the principal handicap to the Allied system of production was not the tonnage lost by enemy action but the wastage of shipping space through inferior management and inaccurate calculations. The stumbling block in the way of better management was the American habit of calculating exclusively in terms of 'sailings' instead of 'tonnage employed'.[14]

The heart of the British contribution was the secretariat operated through the Ministry of War Transport which had been formed from the Mercantile Marine department of the Board of Trade. This department had recruited as temporary civil servants a number of shipowners, lawyers, actuaries, and dons. Their sense of common endeavour led to the production of a major planning tool, the 'shipping budget'. At the Casablanca Conference in January 1943 when Roosevelt and Churchill discussed the principal steps in strategy, it became obvious that shipping space and the availability of assault landing craft were limiting factors in determining the scope of possible operations. After the convoy losses in March 1943, at the next conference between the two leaders in Washington in May the Americans were more amenable to British suggestions for the joint management of shipping. The Combined Shipping Adjustment Board set up in January 1942 had in practice worked two systems in two spheres of influence, British and American. But after May 1943 the value of a common system for 'shipping budgets' was fully realized, and the planning of the invasion of Europe enjoyed better shipping management than earlier operations.

The central apparatus in the allocation of shipping space had its regional counterpart in various supply centres established in different parts of the world. The model for regional planning was the Middle East Supply Centre in Cairo which grew out of the Minister of State's office set up to serve his needs as a Cabinet Minister. This exercise in regional co-ordination with a direct link to the Cabinet began when Lyttelton arrived in Cairo in July 1941. The supply centre was a separate branch of military headquarters with its own director-general responsible to the Minister. It tried as far as possible to use the normal channels of trade, but to control these by an elaborate system of import licences. The Ministry of War Transport in Whitehall was responsible for the supply centre, and was directly in touch with the Anglo-American joint boards, particularly the Combined Shipping Adjustment Board. One of the valuable functions of regional supply centre was liaison with the Ministry of Food in the bulk purchase of overseas foodstuffs for consumption at home.

The centre and the regions

Lyttelton moved from the Middle East Supply Centre to another regional system at home, much less glamourous than the arrangements made for supply and shipping. When he took over as the new Minister of Production in March 1942 a contrast of style and approach was already apparent between the centre and the regional organizations. The latter were inter-departmental committees composed of the representatives of the supply departments and of industry. The Joint War Production Staff which the new ministry put together could only work by persuasion; the administrative controls remained with departments. The new machinery exemplified a moral tale on the difficulty of adding a central programming organization onto existing networks. It never quite overcame the improvisations of the first two years of war; and it was always conscious that there was never going to be the rapid reconversion to peace-time purposes which the United States authorities anticipated.

The contrast between the centre and the regions reflected the difference between central preoccupations and spontaneous reactions in the field. The Joint War Production Staff and their colleagues in Whitehall tended to focus on American statistics, and to search for the imbalances in British contributions to the joint effort. Their work was expressed in terms of capital formation and use, or accumulated skills and deployment. They tended to look ahead to the long-term consequences of departmental sponsorship in industry. The regional boards and their committees were much closer to the day-to-day lives of the working population. Their members applied the rules for allocating government contracts between different firms; they decided what changes were necessary in the direction of labour. The managers and trades unionists involved thought largely in terms of the immediate opportunities created by a temporary suspension of market competition and of the normal rules of collective bargaining. The lessons of the war economy were to be applied then and there, not in the distant future. 'Parent' companies helped others with less experience making the same product; regional chairmen allocated scarce raw materials on their own authority; panels of production engineers helped desingers to simplify their drawings.

Each side of this contrast illustrated the weaknesses of Cabinet government with party discipline removed by coalition. When coalition removes the discipline of party the programming arrangements devised by central committee secretariats paid respect to the predominant role of department organizations, and the vulnerability of all interdepartmental work to the veto of a senior minister reminded those concerned with secretariat business that Cabinets normally imposed a collective view on departments by agreeing a party policy. Both ministers and senior officials had to tread carefully to avoid provoking unnecessary opposition in the special allocation of departmental posts which the prime Minister had devised. The latter's own veto was itself the most difficult obstacle to bypass.

The planning arrangements devised by the regional boards were critically handicapped by the convention of Cabinet government that all interdepartmental disputes could only be settled at Cabinet level. Nevertheless the regional boards were far more effective in marrying departmental organization with representative from all sides of industry than a number of attempts made to provide for a similar representation at the centre. In June 1941 the British Employers' Federation and the TUC had suggested setting up a central advisory committee with twelve representatives from each side. But no moves were made to follow up this suggestion until the Ministry of Production had revised the regional board structure as a whole in the summer of 1942. A new National Production Advisory Council was then formed. The Ministry of Labour already had its own National Joint Advisory Council, established at the outbreak of war, which Bevin reduced to the status of a smaller joint consultative committee. The Reconstruction Secretariat had also created its own advisory panel of employers and industrialists. None of these central bodies was highly regarded.

For the final stages of total mobilization the regional boards were given new full-time controllers who directed the work of their committees. In June 1942 after a long examination of the regional structure by a committee under Sir Walter Citrine the boards were given a new lease of life under new executive committees. These established more effective contact with the regional forms of joint consultation between employers and trades unionists, particularly the joint production committees. The reform of the regional structure raised in an acute form the constitutional difficulty of placing the Minister of Production in the position of an 'overlord' supervising ministers who were technically all responsible to Parliament, each for his own department. This difficulty was surmounted by appointed to each new regional executive committee the heads of each department's regional office—an interdepartmental committee of 'equals' under the chairmanship *not* the direction of a new full-time regional controller from the Ministry of Production. These regional exeuctives had a headquarters counterpart, the Regional Organization Committee, through which all instructions and guidance were channelled.[15]

But it was precisely at the regional level that the sacrifices of accepting coalition government were most acutely felt. The frustrations of industrialists and trade unionists were given voice in the regional consultative committees; the first signs of industrial unrest among coal miners and munition workers were spotted by regional representatives. Bevin was the senior minister who was the most exposed to the expression of popular discontent, and he for his part made clear that he thought the only way to avoid a post-war depression was to keep the system of controls after the war had ended.[16] He wanted management and unions to treat their war-time partnership under administrative control as something from which permanent advantages could be drawn.

Yet the coalition until 1943-4 allowed most of the parties interested in industrial reform to do precisely the opposite of what Bevin recommended—to apply the lessons of the war economy as they happened, without waiting for any planned transition to peace. Bevin himself was frequently out of step with both the TUC and the Parliamentary Labour Party. In October 1941 he had faced TUC hostility for advocating an improvement in the manning of the armed forces at the expense of industry, and he tended to antagonize Citrine, the TUC general secretary. He was often criticized by some Labour MPs for not advancing the cause of increased public ownership, and he deliberately avoided attending the 1943 party conference. His one concession to the idea that the lessons of war should be applied immediately was his sponsorship in the coalition of the Catering Wages Bill which was designed to establish a special commission that could review wages and conditions in the catering industry. Many Conservatives saw this as a partisan attack on any consideration of repealing the Trades Disputes Act, although he tried to get the Prime Minister to agree to an independent inquiry into the case put by the civil service unions.

The most contentious application of war economy lessons to be advocated was the cause of nationalization. In December 1941 forty Labour MPs voted against the government and a third of the party abstained in a Commons division on an amendment which sought to attach the nationalization of transport, coalmining and weapons manufacture to the arrangement made for mobilizing more man-power. The miners' strikes of May-June 1942 also revived the issue of nationalizing the coalmines. Bevin and Dalton as the senior Labour Ministers concerned with the mines sought to effect a form of requisitioning short of outright nationalization, but were overruled by their Cabinet colleagues who secured a regime of controls through regional organization without dispossessing the mine-owners. Each of the major parties in coalition contained groups which were poised to prevent the other taking advantage of war conditions.

It was typical of the production system which the coalition inherited and which the party truce tended to keep within the lines of the different forms of departmental sponsorship that the lessons of the war economy were largely considered within departmental consultative units. Each department of state followed its own inclinations and time-table in reconstruction. Until the creation of the Ministry of Reconstruction in November 1943, the only Cabinet Office secretariat to carry little weight with departments was the Reconstruction Secretariat. Many departments resented its inquiries and saw little need to accede to its requests. Not surprisingly this secretariat was the only central one to have close contact with the regions. During 1941-2 many local associations provided it with their suggestions for reform, but it had no ready means for translating them into the means of departmental action.

It was also typical of the coalition's unwritten assumptions that the three Labour ministers in departments with reconstruction interests should often defend their own civil servants and compete for advantage in interdepartmental combat—Bevin at the Ministry of Labour, Dalton at the Board of Trade, and Morrison at the Home Office. Bevin and Dalton often did not see eye to eye, and Bevin and Morrison were suspicious of each other. All three ministers held their own meetings with the representatives of industry, often duplicating each others' work. The only sign of interdepartmental co-operation at ministerial level was a little mild conspiracy to see whether there was any alternative to the Treasury as the chief planning department after the war.[17] It was for a long time recognized that the department which acquired the Economic Section from the Cabinet Secretariat would enjoy a certain pre-eminence. The Economic Section was the one central secretariat of war production which seemed likely to survive.

All the plans for reconstruction were dominated by the influence of the United States war economy on Britain's future capacity in production and international trade. British war production had depended largely on pre-war equipment and methods. The comparable American effort emphasized how British firms were on the whole both less specialized and more prepared to diversify their product range than their counterparts in the United States. American methods of mass production were much more economical, particuarly when measured in labour costs per unit of production. British armament programmes were based on plans to distribute the labour force instead of the American methods of government grants to restructure the plant capacity. The major gains of capital in Britain were in 'investment industries' such as engineering and chemical products; and the major losses in 'consumption industries' such as textile manufacture and food, drink, and tobacco production.[18] One of the arguments of those who wished to apply 'lessons' immediately was that industry should not be allowed to plan its own location and that government should direct investment to designated development areas.

In return for lend-lease arrangements, the United States wanted some specific benefit—what became known as 'the consideration'—in the form of an international agreement on post-war trade. The American government wanted to compel the British to undertake discussions which might modify the imperial preference system and give advantages to American industry. The Mutual Aid Agreement of March 1942 between the two countries in which Britain made the necessary concessions was subsequently a source of much tension and discussion among British ministers.[19] The 'lessons' to be learnt from the war economy always had to be related to the power of the United States to determine what the international context might be.

Chapter five
Reconstruction and social reform

On strategic questions Churchill frequently acted without consulting his senior Cabinet colleagues; on reconstruction questions they for their part acted without involving the Prime Minister. But the difference between the two actions was painfully apparent. Churchill had the power to put into practice immediately the decisions taken on strategy; ministers who were hard pressed to demonstrate that they had ideas in mind could usually only place their proposals on an agenda for reconstruction which was already overcrowded. A willingness to contemplate the frustrations of delay in implementing social reforms became the test of ministerial stamina for coalition arrangements. By 1944 it had become one of the standard arguments for continuing coalition that only such an all-party agreement would enable the House of Commons to clear the backlog of statutory proposals. The Prime Minister had made it quite clear that he regarded any detailed consideration of social reform as a dangerous diversion of ministerial effort from the main course of the battle.

Only pressure from his Cabinet colleagues compelled Churchill to make a public statement on reconstruction in a broadcast speech of March 1943. He then put forward the idea of a four-year plan to cover the period immediately after the war with Germany had been completed. This plan, he suggested, should be presented by either a coalition or what he then called 'a National Government comprising the best men in all parties'. But the broadcast did not strengthen public confidence in the future, or convince his colleagues that he would himself take further action to secure agreement on social questions. It was largely a device to buy time, until ministers could resolve some of their own differences, particularly on the subject of the Beveridge Report. Churchill declined to appoint a Minister of Reconstruction until November 1943, and for the greater part of that year, Cabinet discussions were split between the Reconstruction Problems Committee and the Reconstruction Priorities Committee. The latter was set up to handle the special questions which emerged from what Beveridge proposed. His report had already divided the Labour Party, and perhaps more important, driven a wedge between Labour back-benchers and Labour ministers in the coalition.

The Beveridge Report set the tone of the debate on reconstruction both inside and outside government, because it posed in an acute form the basic question of what the country would be able to afford in providing public services after the war. Everything seemed to depend on the buoyancy of the nation's post-war economy. Doubts were expressed about the possibility of maintaining the necessary level of national income when there was the risk of unemployment and the danger of overburdening the Exchequer. Churchill jumped at the opportunity to draw a distinction between proposals for change and commitments to future expenditure. The Prime Minister put forward the doctrine that his government could not sanction any major developments in public expenditure without a fresh electoral mandate. This doctrine effectively separated a great deal of proposed legislation from the chances of being put into practice. The cost of the Beveridge proposals therefore became a major handicap to the definition of a coalition policy on reconstruction. The major steps in implementation could only be taken after the war with Germany was over, if Churchill's doctrine were pursued.

There had been a great deal of publicity for Beveridge's scheme even before his report was published in December 1942. In a sense, it was more important for its assumptions and for the implications which its message carried than for its actual contents. Beveridge proposed a unification of the existing schemes of social insurance— health, unemployment, pensions—and a standard benefit for every worker when he was unemployed, in return for paying a weekly flat-rate contribution to the government when he was in a gainful occupation. Beveridge associated insurance with other key changes which fell outside his immediate remit—a national health service, family allowances and the maintenance of full employment. All benefits were to be paid at a subsistence level, although it might take time to build up old age pensions to meet this requirement, and industrial injury benefits were to be adjusted to previous earnings. Instead of seven government departments dealing with cash benefits of various kinds, there was to be a single new Ministry of Social Security.

Beveridge precipitated a difference of opinion inside the coalition by bringing forward what he had to say at the critical moment of popular relief after a 'turn in the tide' of battle at El Alamein. 635,000 copies of his report were sold—a record for Stationery Office publications. His style caught a mood of feeling that the sacrifices of the working population should be rewarded, and gave expression to hopes for the future which had been generated by three years of war deprivation. Politicians became conscious of the more radical character of public opinion. Herbert Morrison saw opportunities for the Labour Party to exploit; Labour back-benchers began to examine the probability of implementing a number of basic reforms while the war was still being fought.

Ironically, by raising the whole question of public expenditure in the post-war economy, Beveridge lessened the likelihood of the coalition itself having an agreed programme of social legislation. Ministers were pushed even more into preparing plans rather than taking action. The Treasury had been given plenty of warning to prepare a case against any extravagant financial commitments; and Churchill had been able to parry the pressure upon him from inside the government to make a number of practical proposals.

The main plank in any coalition platform for reconstruction had to be a commitment to promote a high level of employment. This issue arose directly from the impact of war production on the economy. Manpower planning as the key to mobilization for total war had raised hopes that a post-war depression could be avoided. Ministers and officials were strongly influenced by their recollection of the early 1920s. While Beveridge was conducting his publicity campaign for a social security scheme, the official committee of permanent secretaries on 'internal economic policy' was examining the prospects of post-war industrial investment.

Discussion of the Beveridge report also brought to life the political party organizations in a way which threatened to exaggerate divisions inside the coalition. In May 1943 the Conservative Party held its first conference since 1937. This meeting, which showed how widespread was support for Beveridge among Conservatives, made reference to the Prime Minister's reconstruction broadcast in a manner which implied that action should be taken. In June 1943 the Labour Party annual conference was a series of 'field days' for rallies on questions of social policy. But the delegates brought out into the open for the first time the strength of Labour feeling against the maintenance of the 'electoral truce' which forbade the party to put up candidates at by-elections in Conservative constituencies. Aneurin Bevan said that the main issue was how Labour initiative could be restored to British politics; he thought that pleas for national unity were instruments of political blackmail for the benefit of the Conservatives.

Just as the party organizations were pressing ministers to reach some decisions on social questions, the strategic planners were urging them to consider the full implications of the doctrine of 'Germany first'. By the spring of 1943 with the Allied armies well entrenched in Italy, the commanders in the field in the Far East came to consider what might happen when the war in Europe was finished and yet the war against Japan was still in full swing. The different needs of the two theatres of war raised questions not only of logistics but also of morale. How were the plans for demobilization to be phased? How could interest at home be sustained for sacrifices against a more distant enemy? The idea of a 'two-stage ending'—first Germany and then Japan—had to be married to plans on a different time scale—what came to be known as 'the industrial transition', the period necessary to convert industrial capacity to peace-time production.

From June 1943 onwards the seven or eight senior Labour Cabinet ministers in the coalition ('above the line' in Cabinet Secretariat parlance of salary and status) were extremely exposed to criticism from their party rank and file. Although no Labour minister was implicated in the disclosures, the 'leaks' to the newspapers of Cabinet secrets in July 1943 were symptomatic of both the strains on coalition and the subjects which aroused passion. The *Daily Mail* had got wind of the government's plans for demobilization; the *Western Mail* gave a pre-publication review of the contents of the White Paper on education; and the *Daily Herald* had forecast the changes which the government was to make in war pensions; *The Evening News* knew about cuts in the staff of the Ministry of Labour. From the summer of 1943 onwards there were fewer inhibitions about the public debate of social reform.

The coalition lumbered on to develop a set of domestic policies on the basis of the assumption that 'some kind of National Government' would continue after the defeat of Germany, and of the practical necessity to plan for a 'two-stage ending'. But the content of these policies did not encompass as broad a series of measures as many delegates to the party conferences had hoped. Only the Education Bill gave some cause for optimism. This draft legislation had been prepared by the Board of Education in close consultation with interested parties over the space of two years (1941-3). Butler as President of the Board of Education did not come to consider the attitude of the government as a whole until after these interests had been satisfied.[2] The White Paper on Education was published in July 1943; the Bill which was presented in December had its second reading in January 1944. Apart from this measure, the greater part of legislation prepared on behalf of the coalition touched only on the problems of the 'industrial transition' from war to peace and on the mechanics of demobilization. The housing statutes were seen as a necessary accompaniment to demobilization, and the Town and Country Planning Act of 1944 was a mere shadow of what originally had been envisaged. The most important Acts of Parliament passed in the final year of coalition were those which renewed 'emergency powers' for the transition, and the Distribution of Industry Act 1945 which started the process of managing the economy with a high level of employment.

The Legislation Committee of the Cabinet in drawing up a programme for the parliamentary session 1944-5 tried to distinguish between Bills which technically had to be passed by a certain date to keep regulations in force, Bills which were needed to prosecute the war, and Reconstruction Bills. In this last category the Committee in November 1944 defined the twelve Bills which should be given priority, including those on National Insurance, Industrial Injury Insurances, and a National Health Service, but found that any agreed order of this kind still met with difficulties in the departments themselves which had to overcome considerable resistance from interested parties. The legislative programme became something of a lottery for competing ministers to secure a place which might not then be used.

Conservative and Labour ministers came to a sticking-point largely on questions which involved the expropriation of property or the curbing of privilege. One of the principal reasons for the tame and provisional nature of the Town and Country Planning Act was the objection of Conservative ministers to the proposal that local authorities should have powers to take private land when they were faced with the problems of redeveloping these areas which had been flattened by bombing. Conservatives also objected to any measures which seemed to touch upon an extension of public ownership. Many came to accept the need for a national health service which would require co-operation between private and public authorities, but hesitated to contemplate any large-scale nationalization of public utilities or of coal-mining. Labour ministers for their part with considerable support from the representatives of other parties fought to restrict the extent of Exchequer subsidies to farmers which the Ministry of Agriculture was urging.

Differences between Ministers impeded the progress of preparations for reconstruction at the oficial level. These handicaps were exacerbated by the protracted and acrimonious negotiations with the Americans between the summer of 1942 and the winter of 1944-5 on Article VII of the Mutual Aid Agreement.[3] The reconstruction programme gradually came to take on a more and more official character, as civil servants were left with the task of providing the technical means of demobilization, although it was readily conceded on all sides that the emergency powers assumed by the government in war would still be necessary in peace. The Cabinet agenda in

1944-5 was crowded with the details of redeploying manpower after the defeat of Germany. Norman Brook as the permanent secretary to the Minister of Reconstruction ran what amounted to a separate section of the Cabinet Secretariat for special duties, holding together all the many proposals of the various reconstruction committees.

As the nation's resources were all set to be invested in the Allied invasion of Europe, it looked as if the spirit of the House of Commons for sustaining a coalition was beginning to ebb away. In February 1944 the National Executive Committee of the Labour Party undertook a detailed examination of concrete proposals for breaking the 'electoral truce'. At the beginning of March, Attlee came down heavily in favour of maintaining the existing arrangements which he had suggested in 1941. All three party leaders were to continue signing a general appeal on behalf of the government candidate at by-elections—the candidate of the party whose member had either died or retired. But Attlee's firm stand was not taken without some doubts about the party's future.

Politicians hesitated to come to terms with an electorate which they thought had developed a new range of political interests in the course of the war production effort. It was almost as if they were not quite sure of the degree to which traditional loyalties had been transformed. They agreed to the Speaker's Conference on electoral reform in 1944 as if they wanted a way of exploring what had happened. The Prime Minister's doctrine that the House of Commons required a new electoral mandate before committing the country to extensive social expenditure was by this time being extended to cover the whole range of proposed legislation. By late 1944 a large proportion of the Ministers and officials concerned began to contemplate the prospect of a return to party politics before some outstanding items on the agenda could be settled.

Mobilization and 'war aims'

Churchill had neither the temperament nor the sense of obligation to pursue in social policy the special role which he had defined for himself in stragetic and diplomatic questions. He was not touched by the influence of social studies which had produced a vast literature on social reform during the 1930s, and he had little contact with the exigencies of life among the poorly paid and poorly housed, whose interests were championed by other Ministers such as Attlee and Bevin. His fascination with the application of the chemical and physical sciences to improve weapons technology did not extend to an increased use of social science research. Unlike Attlee and Cripps, he was not involved before the outbreak of war in such research institutes as Political and Economic Planning or the National Institute for Economic and Social Research. Sociological investigation which at Attlee's suggestion was examined in 1944-5 by a Committee on Social Science Research under Sir John Clapham, the economic historian, was an almost completely closed book to the Prime Minister. This was *par excellence* the field of interest which Churchill associated with the name of Beveridge, who had been director of the London School of Economics from 1919 to 1937. The Beveridge Report was no sudden inspiration, but the culmination of a life-time's work in social studies. Beveridge's belief in the principle of social insurance was not just a modest proposal for administrative change but a statement of faith about the proper relationship between the state, the individual, and voluntary organizations.

The Prime Minister was in no hurry to take advantage of the opportunities presented by mobilization for total war in order to introduce permanent measures of social reform. He quite deliberately left as much as possible of 'home front' business to the Lord President's Committee. To give any higher priority to reconstruction questions required a reshuffle of Cabinet posts and a rearrangement of Cabinet committees. Proposals for new legislation were handled directly by the Home Affairs Committee which also reported to the Lord President. The informal meetings of 'home front' ministers—those in charge of departments which were not immediately concerned with either strategy or production—which the Prime Minister instituted in 1942 were designed to keep them informed about the progress of the war, not to give them a sounding board for the discussion of social questions. Reconstruction business was principally confined to the work of junior ministers—Greenwood as Minister without portfolio (1940-2) and Jowitt as Paymaster General (1942-3)—who supervised the Reconstruction Secretariat of the Cabinet Office. Greenwood and Jowitt were both Labour spokesmen, and in the eyes of the Prime Minister their office was to a large extent a safety valve for the release of some of the pressure on the Cabinet as a whole. These ministers had no executive responsibilities and could therefore set their own agenda of investigation and discussion. They were a symbol of the coalition's 'war aims'.

The nation's experience of mobilization provided an agenda which other 'home front' ministers frequently found it difficult to ignore. The morale of the people was strongly influenced by the rhetoric of association between was sacrifice and peace-time reward. Although the Prime Minister's own speeches did not play upon aspirations for a better social order—nationalism was enough—the notion of equality of sacrifice in which all social classes participated was presented in so many different forms that post-war conditions were a constant subject of speculation. When the news was censored about defeat in battle or when pictures which depicted suffering were not allowed to appear, newspapers, books and films tended to give ample space to fantasies. The BBC as the principal guardian of mass communication promoted programmes, such as the broadcasts of J. B. Priestley, which included socialist ideas. Even the panel of experts known as 'the Brains Trust' which answered listeners' questions gave scope for consideration of social reform. *Picture Post* and *Illustrated* included regular articles on social questions. The dispersal of many professional people away from London and the South East to avoid the German bombing helped to stimulate provincial study groups and working parties. The long dark nights of 'the black-out' were passed in argument about the future. The surviving files of the Reconstruction Secretariat are full of 'blueprints' and draft legislation supplied by provincial university professors or adult education classes.

The agenda of social reform contained a number of themes which owed a great deal to the immediate consequences of war-time mobilization. The key note in nearly all of them was the value of 'planning'. Just as the military were dedicated to working out a systematic strategy to encircle Germany, civilian authorities were supposed to apply their minds to the pursuit of peace. In spite of the war-time limitations on book production and the inferior quality of the paper allowed, there were a large number of publications on the feasibility of reconciling the imperatives of planning with the traditions of parliamentary democracy. Labour Party thinkers were themselves stirred to consider what modifications were necessary to the party's programme in the light of the planning concepts put forward in the 1941 budget. Evan Durbin, for example, whose *The Politics of Democratic Socialism* (1940) written in the summer of 1939 had encapsulated all the main elements of 1930s thinking, turned his attentions from the discoveries of modern psychology — democracy as the result of particular people's character — to the techniques of economic analysis. Many socialist thinkers wanted a democratic alternative to the model of planning presented by the Soviet Union whose form of government they refused to follow.

The classic expression of this area of concern was the 1941 Committee from which there sprang a new political party — Common Wealth — the quintessence of 'war aims' discussion. This Committee was a self-styled 'ginger group' which embodied all the strands of war-time polemics — 'Colonel Blimp being pursued through a land of Penguin Specials by an abrasive meritocrat, a progressive churchman, and J. B. Priestley.'[4] The latter was the committee's chairman. Its members included MPs, academics, journalists and publishers. In July 1942 at the time of the fall of Tobruk when the Allied armies seemed close to disaster, the committee was merged with Sir Richard Acland's Forward March movement to form Common Wealth. Acland took over the party's presidency from J. B. Priestley. The immediate appeal of the party was that socialism was necessary to win the war. Its supporters attributed the blunders of strategy and mobilization not to technical incompetence but to the moral failings of capitalist society. The battle of El Alamein destroyed the credibility of this posture, but the party continued to attract followers as Acland expounded his three principles: common ownership, vital democracy, and morality in politics. At the height of its influence, the party had 15,000 members in 300 branches, largely around London and Merseyside, where young professionals and salaried managers wanted to contribute ideas to the debate on social reform.[5] It was never a threat to the Labour Party in working-class areas.

Support for Common Wealth seems to have been directly related to experience in the voluntary organizations which made the best of war-time austerity and in which could be seen all the virtues of co-operation between the classes. The voluntary social services, many of which were staffed by middle-aged and middle-class ladies, such as the Women's Voluntary Service and the Citizen's Advice Bureaux, were given an enormous boost by the sheer scale of the destruction caused by the bombing and the regimentation of evacuated civilians. In the 'people's war' civilians were in the front line; they had to be organized with some precision; they required food, clothing, and shelter—often at a moment's notice. All citizens were bidden by government propaganda to 'make do and mend'— an opportunity for the sewing circles to repair old clothes and make new ones from old scraps; nearly every town and village had its own organization for collecting salvage: waste paper, tins, bottles, an opportunity for consumers to allow manufacturers to recycle their products. The government tapped the money which was not spent by bringing together volunteers for the collection of 'National Savings', and for special efforts such as 'buy a Spitfire' or 'build a battleship'.

In popular opinion, Hitler was given credit for compelling the nation to look again at its social structure. The debate on social questions was conducted against a background of regular obser-vations about the consequences of 'fighting on the home front'. Reconstruction issues were important not only for focusing public attention on the future but also for giving recognition to what was happening. Whenever Attlee had an argument with Churchill about the need for the coalition to reach a number of specific conclusions on reconstruction, he invariably pointed to what had already come to pass, not to what might be achieved when the war was over. Many writers on reconstruction concentrated on what they thought they could already see. Perhaps the most common suggestion was that the evacuation of working-class children from the big towns to the countryside had given the middle classes in general and the professionals handling them in particular a powerful shock about the health and nutrition of poorer families. 'Hitler' had also stopped the building of new houses in the suburbs for the more prosperous. As soon as the older and poorer property in the centre of towns came to be destroyed by enemy action—particularly in London's East End—the contrasts between old and new, poor and prosperous, and centre and periphery, all gave a boost to the idea among modern architects that towns should be properly planned. The 'green belt' of countryside which should be preserved around large towns and the 'garden city' or new town were concepts which were given a fresh lease of life. Even the rather chaotic arrangements for weapons manufacture were interpreted in terms of opportunities for social reform. Industry had adapted itself to the dispersal of factories making different components of the same unit, which was subsequently assembled. Not only did the art of assembling provide a precedent for the erection of prefabricated buildings—the housing shortage after the war was met with 'prefabs'—but also the dispersal of government contracts seemed to have immediate application as a device for channelling government aid to the 'depressed areas'. It is not surprising that the main technical questions on which coalition ministers found they had common ground were the location of industry and housing. Even Churchill in 1944 enjoyed running the Cabinet Committee which he called his 'housing squad'.

Much of the government's agenda for reconstruction came from outside the political parties which supported the coalition. Beveridge was not alone in getting publicity for his ideas, but he was one of the few who were fortunate enough to be given an official vehicle from which to launch them. The supreme irony of the success of the Beveridge Report was that Beveridge had been pushed into becoming Chairman of the Social Insurance Committee in June 1941, because Bevin wished to remove him from the Ministry of Labour where he aspired to becoming the director-general of manpower. As a man who—as he later admitted—had been 'kicked upstairs'[6] he had the opportunity of devoting himself to one of his greatest enthusiasms. Another planner who enjoyed the notoriety of official sanction was Sir Patrick Abercrombie, who was commissioned in 1941 by the London County Council to draw up a master plan for the capital city. He was invited in 1942 by the Minister of Works to extend this into a regional plan for Greater London.

One of the most elaborate research programmes designed to bring together all the different aspects of social policy was that sponsored by Nuffield College, Oxford. In May 1940 the Warden of the College who was then serving as one of the regional commissioners suggested that his colleagues should draw up a scheme of inquiry. When the Fellows considered his proposals they emphasized the need to examine the problems faced by local authorities and voluntary organizations in handling evacuation arrangements and civil defence—the theme was 'post-war England is being made now'. By February and March 1941 a programme was agreen upon and a budget supplied for the recruitment of research assistants[7]. Margery Perham was encouraged to supervise a parallel project on the colonial territories. Officials from the Reconstruction Secretariat advised Greenwood to give his ministerial blessing to the scheme, and the college was commissioned to undertake a number of specific enquiries. By October 1941 the college was welcoming experts to the first of a series of conferences.

To a large extent the political parties followed in the train of publicists and ideologues of various kinds working in the field of social policy, and the House of Commons itself did not devote a large proportion of its time to reconstruction issues until after the Beveridge Report had appeared. But the party organizations were not slow to pick up the principal themes of popular discussion. Even before the coalition was formed during the period of the 'phoney war' both the Conservatives and Labour had party committees looking at future home policy. Butler who was then a parliamentary under-secretary at the Foreign Office was nevertheless involved in a party thinking on domestic affairs long before Churchill moved him to be President of the Board of Education[8]. The Labour Party National Executive Committee met Keynes in May 1940 to discuss his ideas on pay policy. Transport House had issued notes of guidance to speakers on behalf of the Labour Party in March 1940. The party's document produced in January of that year, *Labour and the War,* established the links between home policy and war aims. The Liberal Party in 1940 was the first to establish a number of linked committees on different aspects of post-war policy.

But although it did not retain a large number of agents in the field throughout the war, the Labour Party seems to have kept a greater sense of cohesion for policy discussions than the Conservatives. Churchill after his defeat at the General Election of 1945 accused Labour of having had an organizational advantage, because trades unionists who were often in reserved occupations stayed at home, while Conservative Party agents went into the armed forces[9]. But this advantage was less important than the difference between the parties on basic questions of reform. The Labour Party simply picked up much more effectively all the resonances of expert evidence and social research. It was a natural channel for the expression of hope in the future. The party's national agent, who was evacuated to Market Bosworth in Leicestershire, kept the machine steadily ticking over. Unlike the Conservatives, the party retained its custom of holding an annual conference and of publishing for delegates an annual parliamentary report. In August 1941 it even began a 'book service' for supplying new publications on socialist subjects on lines similar to those followed by the Left Book Club. In 1942 the London Labour Party began organizing a series of lectures on reconstruction themes.

The principal Labour Party committee on reconstruction problems in 1941 had several sub-committees including one called 'the social and economic transformation of Great Britain' under the chairmanship of Emmanuel Shinwell. From these committees the party's principal left-wingers who had not joined the government—Aneurin Bevan, Alice Bacon, Jennie Lee—could stress the importance of trying to persuade the coalition government to bring in socialist measures. Harold Laski, a professor at the London School of Economics, became chairman of the party. His book begun in October 1939 but not finished before the Beveridge Report appeared, *Reflections on the Revolution of our Time* (1943), argued that the continuance of coalition government ought to depend on the terms which Churchill could offer to the Labour Party. In a sentence presumably penned before El Alamein, he wrote (p. 195): 'we cannot win the war unless we make the idea of a more just society a part of the actual policy by which it is won'. He deplored the tendency to think of reconstruction as an 'after-war' problem instead of 'a process determined by the methods by which war waged' (p. 156). The vice of all coalitions he believed was 'postponement'.

The Conservative Party organization had no comparable propagandist. The local associations in the constituencies were kept in some order, but they lacked Labour's interests to follow through the debates on social policy which were being conducted in research groups outside the parties. The Conservative committee on postwar problems set up in 1941 under Butler does not seem to have made as much impact on party opinion as the Tory Reform Committee of thirty-six Conservative MPs under the chairmanship of Lord Hinchingbrooke. This committee was set up in March 1943 and was the direct product of an increasingly partisan House of Commons. Its members came together as a result of the split in party ranks when voting on Bevin's Catering Wages Bill. These Conservatives thought it important that the party should turn to social reform and attempted to persuade their parliamentary colleagues to support an extension of the coalition's work for reconstruction. They were, however, in the awkward position of proposing an adoption of the Beveridge recommendations from the government benches when the most vociferous clamour came from 'the official opposition'. The latter consisted almost entirely of Labour back-benchers. The Tory reformers faced the impossible task of converting their party from the inside.

Labour Ministers on the government benches felt vulnerable to the attacks of those Labour back-benchers who chose to sit opposite. Attlee tried to make it clear that Labour had not joined the coalition to secure socialist legislation but to promote a national victory. There were, nevertheless, many awkward moments when Labour supporters expected to gain from Labour's presence in the coalition; and such occasions became more frequent after the open disagreements about the Beveridge Report. Indeed, there had from the beginning of the coalition been a fear among Labour ministers that they would be accused of 'MacDonaldism'—splitting the party by forming a 'National government' with the Conservatives as Ramsay MacDonald had done in 1931. Chuter Ede, the Labour parliamentary secretary at the Board of Education, warned Attlee in February 1941 that 'a minority of the party are trying to recreate the position of 1929 and 1931.[10] Labour ministers from time-to-time had meetings to discuss the problems which seemed pertinent to their special position, although it was frequently difficult to find the time for such party activities within the very pressing timetables of departmental life.[11] They also attended occasional meetings of the National Council of Labour which brought together representatives of the TUC General Council, the co-operative movement, the National Executive Committee, and the Administrative Committee in the House of Commons which organized the 'official opposition'.

Bevin was perhaps the most provocative minister in the eyes of the back-benchers who disagreed with the coalition's policy on Beveridge, and Morrison the most conciliatory. Attlee and Dalton tried to steer the party away from confrontations. After the back-bench vote against the government in February 1943 Bevin refused to attend party meetings including the important party conference of that year. Morrison became the sole ministerial representative on the committee drafting a report on future policy for that conference, and although he was fairly discreet in his public speeches, he annoyed Churchill by giving speeches on reconstruction questions. The party re-established its policy committee after the 1943 conference, with Dalton as chairman, and began to extend its consultations with the TUC with the purpose of defining policy questions before the next General Election. Such consultations marked the run-up to Labour's withdrawal from the coalition. By September 1944 the party secretary was in a position to bring together the different discussions in order to construct an election manifesto.

The most striking evidence of the gap between the Labour leadership and its rank and file in the country was the defeat of the National Executive Committee at the 1944 conference. The rebellious back-benchers had more support outside the House of Commons than Labour ministers realized. The main issue in December 1944 was the degree to which the party should declare its determination to nationalize a number of key industries. Dalton's policy committee had been somewhat equivocal. Its report on full employment led the platform to propose a form of words which referred only to the 'transfer to the state of power to direct the policy of our main industries'. But conference delegates from the floor voted in favour of the resolution sponsored by the Reading Trades Council which called for the public ownership of 'land, large-scale building, heavy industry, and all forms of banking, transport and fuel and power'.[12]

But the Labour leadership would never have stayed in the coalition if it had attempted to respond to party pressure. Paradoxically, it was important for Labour to be in government but not to show its policy inclinations too overtly: Conservatives would have been compelled to behave in more partisan manner if all the calls for change had come from the Labour side of the coalition. As it was, Labour ministers kept their bargain with the Prime Minister, and at the same time benefited from the groups outside Parliament (and some outside the party) which set the pace of discussions on reconstruction. Conservative ministers had neither the same embarrassments nor the same advantages on questions of social reform. They were under no obligation to satisfy the party rank and file. Nor was there 'an official Conservative opposition'.

Churchill himself was more vulnerable to party criticism than the Conservative ministers he appointed. He was particularly exposed to the fears expressed by Conservatives about the influence exercised by Labour through the sheer holding of office. Some Conservatives were continuously on the alert for any signs of what they regarded as illegitimate ministerial behaviour. Dalton, the

Labour leader whom Churchill had transferred to the Board of Trade in February 1942, was the object of many Conservative suspicions, as he occupied such a key post in the designation of future policy for industry. The prospect of post-war planning by government in order to regulate the market prompted a Conservative back-lash against the continuation of the coalition. Dalton on entering the Board of Trade quickly became embroiled in a dispute on the future of the coal industry because the Mines Department fell into his portfolio. He asked Beveridge to conduct an inquiry into coal stocks and announced the introduction of coal rationing. Many Conservatives saw in his plans a back-door method of presenting nationalization to the mine-owners. Dalton was subsequently under a regular attack from Conservative industrialists whenever he seemed to stray from what they regarded as the coalition's remit.

Reconstruction questions tempted many Conservatives to re-assess the value of having Churchill as party leader, and to try to persuade him to resist the pressures for state intervention in the management of the economy. During 1942-3 as the House of Commons itself fell into a more partisan style of debate, various groups were formed outside Parliament to promote 'free enterprise' after the war. Conservatives took up the cause championed by Hayek in *The Road to Serfdom* published in 1944 which associated economic planning with a special kind of bureaucratic tyranny. In the autumn of 1942, a small pressure group called 'Aims of Industry' was founded. This was followed by such groups as the National League for Freedom started in April 1943. As the publicity in favour of planned social reform grew, a number of counter-proposals were promulgated. The publisher, Sir Ernest Benn, who had opened the Individualist Bookshop in 1925 and started the weekly newspaper *The Independent,* began publishing books in a new 'Liberty Library' series in January 1941. After a number of meetings in 1941-2 he launched the 'Manifesto of British Liberty', and began the 'Society of Individualists' at a special dinner. Ralph Assheton who became the chairman of the Conservative party in 1944 thought that Hayek's book should be sent by the 'individualists' to fifty leading socialists.[13]

But Churchill resisted the blandishments of his own party. Indeed, some Conservatives thought that in making his broadcast in March 1943 on a four-year reconstruction plan he had given way to the socialists in his government. Labour ministers were always being characterized as the source of social reform initiatives. The practice of the coalition was for the Prime Minister to procrastinate on reconstruction issues while the representatives of different groupings tried to capture his attention. Most of the time Churchill appears to have favoured any action which might promote the continuation of the coalition, but he also occasionally toyed with the idea of leading a partisan administration. It was almost as if to keep a balance that Churchill brought Beaverbrook back into his Cabinet in September 1943 just before appointing Woolton to be the Minister of Reconstruction, a long awaited appointment. Both Labour ministers and Tory reformers had feared that Churchill might give responsibility for reconstruction to Beaverbrook. The latter was strongly opposed to retaining a coalition. By having Beaverbrook as Lord Privy Seal and Woolton as Minister of Reconstruction Churchill kept his options open a little longer.

The transition to peace

The strongest force in driving the coalition to act collectively on home policy questions was the need to disentangle the vast collection of special war-time regulations as soon as peace returned, and this force also compelled ministers to decide whether there was a case for retaining such regulations during whatever 'transition' was envisaged. By 1943 it was obvious that almost any set of discussions on home policy could not avoid touching on the uncertainties of what the military called 'post-hostilities planning'. While nothing was properly settled about the range of issued raised by demobilization, ministers could hardly devote themselves to working out the details of reconstruction which the subjects required and which many authors in books and newspapers were regularly demanding. Churchill seemed reluctant to give a lead, even on the technical question of revising defence regulations.

When the major step was at last taken in November 1943 with the creation of the Ministry of Reconstruction, which provided the basis for a degree of co-ordination and for defining a coalition legislative programme, there was the additional difficulty of deciding how to relate Britain's anticipated weakness in international finance to the formulation of a set of home policies. The Reconstruction Committee of the Cabinet was established after an informal discussion among senior ministers, who asked the Prime Minister to agree to a second and entirely separate committee on 'post-war financial and economic policy in the international field'.[14] The Committee on Reconstruction was deliberately excluded from touching all the important questions of external economic policy. As ministerial discussions progressed, one of the major differences of opinion to emerge was on the question of how to replace the Lord President's Committee after the war. Should there be two committees, one on national development and the other on overseas economic policy?

Senior civil servants, although many of them were quite glad to resist what they regarded as an excess of zeal among those politicians and authors who had joined the march to the millenium of reconstruction, were nevertheless frustrated when the Prime Minister refused their advice on questions of machinery. Churchill's tight control over the disposition of ministerial offices limited what could be done. For example, he regularly declined the suggestion that he should appoint a Minister of Planning. Although he eventually agreed to add responsibility for physical planning to the office of the Ministry of Works, he was not prepared to give the scope to the town planning movement which a separate department would have created. In the Cabinet reshuffle in February 1942, Bridges tried to persuade him that he should appoint a Minister for Reconstruction who would then work under the direction of the Lord President but with his own Cabinet Committee. Bridges's idea of this committee was that it should handle what he saw as all three aspects of reconstruction—social questions, physical planning and external economic policy.[15] In spite of Churchill's refusal to take this advice, the Cabinet Committee on Reconstruction Problems established an inter-departmental committee to consider setting up a 'central planning authority' which without any major change in the law could supervise the rebuilding of bombed towns and the improvement of the nation's stock of houses. Such an authority would have been similar to the 'national development executive' proposed by Greenwood in 1941 before he was excluded from the Cabinet in the reshuffle.

Cripps during his period of office as Lord Privy Seal and Leader of the House of Commons was naturally the recipient of many suggestions for improving the machinery of government and for settling the major questions which had to precede any legislative programme on home policy. He succeeded in getting Cabinet to set up a machinery of government committee, but not without facing the Prime Minister's personal opposition. It is doubtful whether Churchill would ever have acceded to this request if there had not been a general feeling among ministers and senior civil servants that reconstruction raised some peculiarly difficult questions of administrative machinery. The Prime Minister was finally persuaded by the combined weight of Anderson and Wood. Cripps was much less successful during his brief period of ascendancy in getting Cabinet to decide some of the major issues of policy. G. D. H. Cole, who was the principal director of research in the Nuffield College Reconstruction Project, told Cripps in April 1942 that:

no plans will get made until the Government officially announces that it proposes to follow after the war a long-term policy of full employment without deflation, increasing public expenditure to offset slumps, that it has in view a long-term programme of building and civil engineering on a large scale, and that it proposes to go ahead with a big development of the public utility services under public ownership and control

It was characteristic of the tensions created in reconstruction arguments that the Nuffield College Survey withdrew its support from official civil service research before the Beveridge Report was published. Just before that report appeared, Cole in November 1942 had recommended to his research workers that they should cease to supply material to government departments. The difficulty with policy research as they saw it was that 'work necessarily cuts right across departmental frontiers.'[16] While the Beveridge Committee was sitting and while all the alternatives for a 'central planning authority' were being considered, research workers outside government found that departments wished to place restrictions on what they could do.

The problems of outsiders were a direct product of a deliberate policy to leave reconstruction questions primarily to departments. In the absence of any strong sense of policy objectives within the coalition there was no real alternative to work at the official level on a departmental basis, developed or discarded according to the interests of individual ministers. Greenwood recognized this unpalatable fact from the beginning. The Cabinet Committee on War Aims decided in October 1940 that there was no need to employ a large staff. Greenwood made it clear in his dealings with other ministers that his Reconstruction Secretariat existed only to co-ordinate the many studies which were necessary; he attached importance to keeping detailed investigations into a particular subject concentrated in the responsible department.[17]

Some ministers revelled in the freedom to make their own departmental plans for reconstruction. Hugh Dalton, for example, on becoming President of the Board of Trade in February 1942, began to look for talent to staff what he called his 'post-warriors' or post-war planners. By October 1942 the department had established its own reconstruction committee and got together a sufficient number of qualified people to start its own 'internal reconstruction' department. During the same summer the Foreign Office decided to employ Gladwyn Jebb on reconstruction, and the Colonial Office created a research committee with Lord Hailey in the chair and a special full-time secretary.

The staff of the Reconstruction Secretariat often complained of this exclusion from departmental investigation. Indeed, they thought they they normally had little to do with the many 'pledges' made by ministers on individual questions of policy. Their principal weakness was that they could not rely on receiving an automatic invitation to sit on interdepartmental committees or listen to interdepartmental discussions. They were not, for example, represented in 1942 on the sub-committees set up by the committees of permanent secretaries to discuss future problems in both domestic and international finance. The job of co-ordinating departmental plans went by the board because the secretariat had neither the strength nor the support to create the appropriate liaison. One member of staff in January 1943 suggested that it should 'pick the lions from Chatham House, Nuffield, and PEP' in order to mobilize the most suitable talent.[18] But at this date the only way of bringing together different departmental approaches to the same problems was to exploit the 'home front' powers of the Lord President and the 'home front' responsibilities of the Lord President's Committee. The trouble was that the office and committee which handled the application of war regulations could hardly spend the time to consider their future significance.

The story of reconstruction policy consists therefore before 1943 largely of a number of different departmental accounts, each with its own emphasis on the problems to be treated and the interests to be consulted. Each department had been encouraged by the system of control over raw materials to see itself as the 'sponsor' of particular industries; the guide to 'production authorities' published by the Ministry of Production was a list of the major points of contact between Whitehall and its many industrial clients. Departments outside the industrial field, such as the Board of Education and the Ministry of Agriculture, had similar sets of pressure groups of their own. The war did a great deal to formalize the processes of consultation between government and organized interests. It became almost axiomatic that any given group should have its departmental advocate.

The principal exceptions to this rule were local authorities which feared that they might be displaced by central agencies in any programme of social reform, and statutory undertakers, such as the suppliers of gas and electricity, which prided themselves on their direct access to Parliament without coming under any central or local control, and were afraid of proposals to limit their freedom of action. One of the fundamental questions of reconstruction was whether the provision of social services could continue to follow the many different combinations of central and local government. The Nuffield College Reconstruction Survey was not the only group to put local government reform high on its priorities for action;

other study groups pressed for a full-scale reconsideration of local authority areas and functions. The regionalization of central department work had also drawn attention to the different standards of local authorities. The country had been divided into fifteen civil defence regions, each with a regional commisioner to whom departments had devolved duties. Local authorities saw such officials exercising direct control over their activities by emergency regulation. The Reconstruction Secretariat in the summer of 1941 asked Sir William Jowitt to investigate the impact of regionalization on local government. There were so many strong suspicions and so many rumours about possible government action during 1942-3 that almost the first definite commitment in the coalition's collective deliberation on home policy was the Prime Minister's announcement in September 1943 that local government would not be weakened. Those who had argued that the creation of new units of local government was a pre-requisite of social reform had henceforward to hope that the government would at least agree to some modifications in local government boundaries. Statutory undertakers, such as gas and electricty companies, were not so successful as local authorities in resisting investigation; being less well organized than the local authority associations, they were obliged to agree to modifications of their rights to use the property they owned and their access to Parliament for private bills.

The principal turning point in getting departments to work together on reconstruction and social reform was the decision of the Lord President's Committee in June 1943 to set up an official committee under Sir Claud Schuster of the Lord Chancellor's Department to review all the emergency legislation which the government had used to mobilize people and control resources. The committee, which first met in July but did not get down to hard work until October 1943, was required to devise a programme for dismantling this legislative apparatus and in so doing to consider what might be required for the 'transition'. Part of the force behind getting the Prime Minister to agree to appoint a Minister of Reconstruction was the request of this committee that he should sign a directive requiring all departments to make accurate returns of their statutory powers, and statements of those which they would like to be preserved for reconstruction purposes.

Woolton's appointment as Minister of Reconstruction was announced on 12 November as Churchill boarded a battleship to sail to Egypt where he was due to meet Roosevelt. At the same time, Parliamentary Counsel on whom the burden of legislative drafting would fall begged to be given some indication of the government's order of priorities. He feared that the only indication he would receive of the changes in the law which were required would be the strongest departmental voices. All the officials concerned anticipated a long queue of Bills for Parliament's attention.

Any distinction between legislation which was technically necessary in order to disband the administrative controls and that which politically was desirable in order to meet the expectations of a return to peace had to be made in the context of the Treasury doctrine that it would be a mistake to enact laws which called for greater public expenditure before the aggregate national income and balance of trade after the war could be assessed. Getting rid of controls would save money for the Exchequer, but adding new social services would increase its commitments. The publication of the Beveridge Report had brought the issue to a head in December 1942, and there was still not agreement between ministers in November 1943 when the new Ministry of Reconstruction began work. It was hardly possible to reach agreement when so much seemed to depend on what the United States would allow. Treasury officials who administered the purchase of war material through American lend-lease arrangements were particularly sensitive to the possibilities of a post-war collapse in confidence. They brought their views to bear on the Chancellor of the Exchequer, Wood, until his death in September 1943, and then on his successor, Anderson.

But legislative proposals were not normally discussed only in terms of their estimated costs to the Exchequer. The conduct of the war placed such a tremendous pressure on the Cabinet that it lacked the necessary motives to construct a financial view of domestic policy. The convention developed that any legislative proposal which secured the approval of the appropriate Cabinet Committee could be sent to the Legislation Committee in order to give the Leader of the House and the government Whips sufficient warning of the parliamentary time that would be required for its debate. The Lord President's Committee before November 1943 was the major standing committee to consider departmental proposals. Items were only taken to the War Cabinet if they were politically controversial. The Reconstruction Committee after November 1943 became the most important standing committee for domestic policy and social reform questions. The official steering committee on post-war employment, which began work in July 1943 in the context of the discussions of the Reconstruction Priorities Committee working for the Lord President, presented its findings to the Reconstruction Committee in April 1944. These findings which became the government's White Paper on employment policy went from the latter committee to the Cabinet. Less important matters were handled lower down.

The composition of the Reconstruction Committee was an eloquent testimony to the relatively disproportionate influence of Labour ministers in social policy. Four of its ten members were Attlee, Bevin, Morrison and Jowitt. Their Conservative counterparts were Butler, Lyttelton, Cranborne and Crookshank, with Woolton as the ministerial chairman and Anderson as Chancellor of the Exchequer playing the role of Treasury spokesman and cross-benchmind. The sub-committees of this standing committee sometimes gave an even more prominent place to Labour Ministers. For example, the sub-committee on industrial problems, which later under the 'caretaker administration' in June 1945 became a standing committee on home affairs, consisted of Bevin and Dalton (Labour) and Woolton and Lyttelton (Conservative).

Some Conservative MPs became suspicious of the alleged influence of Labour ministers and reacted against the Tory reform Group in their own party. The Progress Trust, a group of Conservative MPs under Sir Spencer Summers who wished to reduce the party's reform commitment, was founded in November 1943. Churchill himself became suspicious of 'socialist politicians' of such eminence in a position to make specific proposals in Standing Committees. By February 1945 there had been such a build-up of tension between ministers from the two major parties on reconstructions questions that the Prime Minister was prepared to believe in a degree of 'socialist conspiracy'. He thought that Bills were getting on to the legislative agenda of the coalition without any proper sanction from the War Cabinet as a whole, and asked the Legislation Committee to examine the basis of a minister's obligation to consult with his colleagues.

In so far as there was a reconstruction programme for the coalition, it consisted of what could be approved by the Reconstruction Committee without one set of its ministerial members— usually the Conservatives—deciding to 'put the boot in'. Many government statements which appeared during 1944-5 were the products of compromise at this level. Nearly all the major questions of social policy came before this committee in that year. Its members strove to find agreement wherever possible on what seemed to be the most crucial stages in the 'reconversion' of industry. Dalton, although not a member of the committee, as President of the Board of Trade was in regular attendance because so many major subjects came under the aegis of this department. Labour ministers tried hard not to provoke their Conservative colleagues. Attlee thought it wise to persuade Churchill that Cherwell should serve on the committee in his own right. There was always a danger before this appointment was made that the Prime Minister would require Cherwell to put obstacles in the way of what the committee was doing. Brook as Woolton's permanent secretary presided over a series of official committees and sub-committees which also took care not to provoke ministerial antagonism.

Legislative proposals which were considered technically necessary were more easily handled and approved in these reconstruction committees than those which ran the risk of provoking party controversy. The most important element in technical preparations for the 'transition' was the Supplies and Services Bill. As so many of the key regulations for controlling raw materials and food supplies on an annual renewal by Parliament of the emergency powers, the coalition had to commit itself to retaining a number of controls on a more permanent basis for the immediate period after the war was over. Everyone agreed that it would be ridiculous to remove controls at once. The questions were all about which regulations and for how long. It was hoped that the 'transition' could be managed by administrative action with as little statutory change as possible. But the questions raised became so technically complex that the final version of the Bill was not completed before the coalition began to show signs of strain, although the coalition had originally agreed to keep a core of regulations in force for two years (1945-7), Churchill's caretaker administration reduced the period to six months, an action which provoked the new Labour government to impose a five-year period (1945-50).

The other areas of policy in which statutory provision was sometimes technically required were those designed to meet the arrangements for demobilization and the obligations of international agreements. The latter did not come within the terms of reference of the Reconstruction Committee but were nevertheless seen to raise issues of importance for social policy, particularly when they impinged on finance and industry. All the committee members kept an eye on the work of the proposed United Nations and its agencies, such as UNRRA which concerned itself with the rehabilitation of Europe. Demobilization was a direct responsibility of the Reconstruction Committee. It dealt with such questions as the reinstatement of military personnel in civilian employment, the opportunities to be given to the disabled, and the provisions for further education and retraining. Bevin did his best to keep all the main decisions within this field to the care of the Ministry of Labour and National Service. That department from the beginning of the work of its committee on demobilization in late 1942 had associated the planning required with what it saw as the necessity for its own minister to have full responsibility for employment policy as soon as peace arrived.[19] Both Bevin and his civil servants saw demobilization planning as an opportunity to assert the newly found strength of the department.

Proposals for reconstruction were still being argued out primarily in departments, not in Cabinet Committees. The departments best placed to secure priority in the legislative programmes of 1943-4 and 1944-5 were those which enjoyed a fairly self-contained set of functions and had a minister who was prepared to engage with the principal interest groups in his field of responsibilities, in order to draft post-war plans carrying a general consensus. It was even easier to get a place in the programme if what was proposed did not involve an immediate call on public expenditure after the war. Butler forged ahead as President of the Board of Education in getting all interests and parties to agree to a Bill which would make free secondary education available to all, partly because he was able to convince his colleagues that the costs of this reform would accumulate only gradually and not involve a vast and immediate capital outlay. Hudson as Minister of Agriculture, although he had a very clearly defined set of functions, provoked a lot of opposition from other departments precisely because he wanted farmers to have guaranteed prices for farm produce during a stated number of years by means of state subsidies. Those who said that the nation could not afford £86 million for Beveridge's social insurance plans could not stomach £50 million in the pockets of the National Farmers' Union. The controversy was handled largely through the Lord President's Committee during the course of two years (1942-4) and lent a special emphasis to the British position on post-war trade in discussions with the Americans. In April 1944 the farmers were finally told that they were to have guaranteed prices until 1948. Oliver Stanley as Secretary of State for the Colonies stood somewhere between Butler on education and Hudson on agriculture in his request for resources on colonial development. Although his department had been compelled by the war-time regulation of trade, transport, and investment in the Empire to deal much more with other Whitehall departments than it had done before 1939, he still had a degree of autonomy in designing aid to colonies, even if he had to work with the other overseas departments when major questions of international diplomacy were involved. He secured agreement to a commitment of resources for post-war development by getting approval for his Colonial Development and Welfare Bill.

Departments which had no clear set of functions, but relied on securing agreement with other agencies even for fairly modest changes, had more difficulty in getting through the Reconstruction Committee apparatus; some proposals even involved the setting up of new departments. It was the apparent advantage gained by departments which had already developed a strong sense of sponsorship for particular interest groups that led both Ministers and officials to reconsider the allocation of functions between ministerial portfolios; and also partly the need to decide what to do with those departments which owed their existence to war-time regulations alone. The statutes setting up the Ministry of Town and Country Planning and the Ministry of Fuel and Power found their place in the reconstruction programme, but before the coalition broke up no agreement had been reached on constructing a general statute which would permit the executive to transfer functions between departments by statutory instrument. The Labour Government secured such an Act in 1946.

The main areas in which the Reconstruction Committee and its satellites constructed some kind of social policy from departmental proposals were in the field of Beveridge's own activities. The symbols of this policy lay in three major White Papers of 1944—employment, social insurance, and health. The White Paper on employment policy was a document full of qualifications and compromises. It committed the government to retaining certain physical controls over the economy in order to reduce any unemployment caused by the switch from war-time to peace-time production, but it explicitly ruled out any stimulation of demand if there were a depression, by a government-planned deficit for the budget. Neither the left of the Labour Party nor the academic economists who followed Keynes were happy with the final draft of this document. Its main achievement was not technical but symbolic. The government—and therefore whichever party won the next General Election—would have to try to maintain 'a high and stable level of employment after the war'. The White Paper on social insurance in September 1944 finally brought together all the fruits of official discussions on the implementation of the Beveridge Report. This White Paper showed that the Conservatives had reacted favourably to Beveridge when he advocated family allowances and the principle of universal contribution to old age pensions, but had grave doubts about provision of unemployment insurance payments at a full subsistence level. Family allowances—payments to mothers with young children—were a reform which had the full backing of senior ministers; unemployment benefits were much more controversial. The White Paper on a proposed national health service had no serious chance of being translated into a piece of social legislation by the coalition, in spite of the many hours spent by the Ministry of

Health on its preparation. The British Medical Association objected to the idea that free services should be available to all. The Ministry's plans were in fact derived from a mixture of pre-war proposals from that Association to improve hospital services, and war-time experience in the Emergency Medical Service. The latter commandeered hospitals for its own use, and employed doctors and nurses with salaries paid by the government; it therefore for the first time brought together organizations which had previously been paid either by local authorities or by private foundations. The benefits of a more integrated administrative system were so obvious that few believed it would be possible to reinstate the pre-war system. It seemed likely that some new form of health authority would be set up without creating too strong a sense of expropriation among the voluntary agencies.

It was even more difficult to secure agreement whenever the issue of public ownership was raised. Just as the Emergency Medical Services demonstrated clear advantages in the health services, so the state management of the coal mines prompted many to speculate on a contination of centralization after the war. The Labour Party was naturally inclined to argue that the changes in the structure of the mining industry which many engineers thought were urgently needed could best be secured by nationalization. The Conservative side of the Reconstruction Committee could not stomach any move in that direction. Similarly, the plans laid for town and country planning were handicapped by the debate between those who wanted a comprehensive approach which included some expropriation of property by public authorities and those who were happy to proceed in stages. Churchill wanted a planning Ministry which could compel recalcitrant local authorities, but not powers of compulsory purchases. The legislation necessary to create the Minister of Town and Country Planning was initiated before there was any agreement on the principal statute which conferred powers upon him. The Uthwatt report which recommended in 1942 that public authorities, not the private owner, should be allowed to take the 'development value' which accrued from planning decisions, aroused the deepest divisions of opinion within the coalition. The Reconstruction Committee considered how private owners might be compensated for the loss of 'development value'.

The greatest achievement of the Reconstruction Committee was that it provided a basis for the reconversion of industry to peacetime purposes, and particularly to the export trade. Not surprisingly the reconversion had to follow a series of compromises, but officials at least thought they had a sufficiently clear remit to set in motion the necessary machinery. In 1945 at the time of the 'caretaker administration' Bridges felt confident that the policy outlined in the 1944 White Paper on employment would be followed by whichever party won the election, and he prepared for the new government's requirements on that assumption. The Board of Trade, which toyed with the proposal to set up an Industrial Commission, a body of experts to stand as a 'buffer' between government and industry and to advise on aid to individual firms, found so many difficulties in the way of this kind of machinery that it was inclined to concentrate on regional policy and the promotion of exports. The most typical policy instruments to emerge from these discussions were the 'development certificate', a means of licensing factory construction in certain areas, and the credit guarantee for exporters. The Board of Trade also handled the setting up of companies to loan capital to small firms, such as Finance Corporation for Industry, and the Industrial and Commercial Finance Corporation. All these topics were subjects on which the Reconstruction Committee could agree.

The only blemish on the general determination of ministers to find some common ground for industrial growth were the activities of some members of Churchill's entourage who tried to prod him into a more reactionary stance. Beaverbrook and Bracken were considered by many Labour ministers to be largely responsible for the Prime Minister's occasional intransigence. They were widely regarded as responsible for the tone of Churchill's opening electioneering broadcast on 4 June 1945 when he said that the socialists if they came to power 'would have to fall back on some form of Gestapo'. In fact, Churchill alone penned that speech.[20] Attlee earlier in the year while the coalition was still in being had made a strong attack on the interference of Beaverbrook and Bracken in Reconstruction Committee business. He pointed out that they had no direct departmental responsibilities and that they were not inclined to devote the serious attention to reconstruction subjects which these required.[21] The implication of this dispute between the Prime Minister and his deputy was that such ministers at least succeeded in delaying decisions if not in creating havoc in reconstruction planning. Perhaps too much attention during 1944-5 was paid to the susceptibilities of individual ministers.

The value of coalition

The greatest fear among ministers was that their own party would become associated with the necessary but unpopular task of maintaining controls in peace-time in order to ease the process of transition. Coalition by 1943-4 came to be seen partly as a protection against the unrealistic demands of popular expectation. In submitting a brief on the final version of the Supplies and Services Bill to the Chancellor of the Exchequer a Treasury official in April 1945 commented that such an enactment was 'essentially one for a government of all parties.'[22] Civil servants feared the ideological arguments and suspicions which they thought would be engendered if such a Bill were introduced by a single-party government. These fears turned out subsequently to have been thoroughly justified.

Ministers in each major party were happy to leave open as long as possible the questions of when the next General Election would be held and whether the coalition would continue. Morrison at one stage during 1943 even went so far as to suggest that the three major parties should agree on a minimum programme but then go to the country as separate organizations which appealed to voters on the partisan basis of what priorities and additions might be declared. The agreement for such an election campaign would have included a commitment to remain a coalition of parties which would have determined its policies according to the composition of the House of Commons. The principle was that of a national coalition. Labour leaders were not confident that they could win an overall majority, even after the West Derbyshire by-election in February 1944. While the Labour rank and file pressed for an end to the 'electoral truce', their ministers hesitated to throw off the cloak of coalition.

Ministers thought that the electorate might be both unrealistic and unreasonable precisely because it was not equipped, as they were, to see the conflicting demands of social policy and international obligation. Attlee was not anxious to break up the coalition while there was still a chance that an agreed minimum social policy could be combined with a bipartisan approach to foreign affairs. Attlee himself was particularly interested in the link between home and foreign affairs provided by international co-operation in science. He thought that many technological improvements in industry and the resulting growth of the nation's wealth would be the product of government-sponsored scientific projects.

Ministers sensed that the war-weariness of the electorate might encourage even more unrealistic demands for rapid social reform. The build-up of force for the D-Day landings in Normandy was accompanied by the hope that once the invasion had begun there would be a rapid end to the fighting. At the beginning of 1944 it was widely expected that the war in Europe would be over by Christmas. The final assault on Hitler's Germany might lead to a series of spontaneous uprisings by the people of German-occupied countries.

Ministers were also aware of latent discontent among those who had been conscripted for civilian work. With the prospect of a return to peace individuals began to look around for jobs. The Civil Service in April 1944 had to bring in a control of employment order under emergency regulations in order to keep temporary staff at their desks while the tasks of the 'transition' were completed. Some key temporary administrators, such as university teachers and other professionally qualified specialists, began to look for openings in higher education for the academic session 1944-5, or at the latest 1945-6. A committee was established to regulate the release of university teachers from the higher civil service. Ministers noted an increase in absenteeism in both the administration and industry. Managers found it increasingly difficult to hold their temporary work-forces together. By September 1944 the fifth anniversary of the outbreak of war emphasized the anguish and the tedium. The whole population which wanted some sense of release was extremely vulnerable to the weapon which Hitler hoped would sap civilian morale—the pilotless rocket bomber with an engine which cut out over major city centres bringing another wave of destruction comparable with the 'blitz' of 1940-41. These flying bombs, nicknamed 'doodlebugs', began falling on London only ten days after D-Day, and they continued to fall in various more refined versions until after the Allies had crossed the Rhine into Germany in late March 1945. The last campaign in Europe seemed interminably long; the German counter-offensive through the Ardennes in December 1945 was a great blow to the hopes for an early end to the war.

It was remarkable that the industrial unrest which made itself felt was so easily contained. In the spring of 1944 as absenteeism began to increase, there was also a number of attempts to foment strike action, particularly in Yorkshire, Tyneside and Clydeside. Bevin as Minister of Labour was prepared to use defence regulations to break strikes, and was widely criticized in the Labour movement.

When the authorities managed the news and when opinion polls were taken primarily to test the state of civilian morale, it was difficult for ministers to be sure about the trends of public opinion. There is little evidence that the 'White Paper chase' of 1944 aroused much popular enthusiasm. The nuances and ambiguities of the government's statement on employment policy were lost when it was translated into journalistic terminology. The undertaking to maintain a high level of employment could not be presented as a popular gesture, as it would have been if it had come from a party government. The polls taken by the Ministry of Information indicated that people were primarily interested in employment, housing and health policies in their general desire to return to peace as quickly as possible. Such evidence as there was of a swing of opinion towards the Labour Party could not be related to a widespread knowledge of where that party differed from its opponents on social questions. In so far as the electorate were turning to Labour, ministers saw its mood as a general desire for change from war-time austerity. What they could not openly mention was their own profound pessimism about the prospect of Britain securing a rapid rate of industrial expansion as soon as Germany was defeated. Britain was not going to be bargaining from strength, in international diplomacy or trade, whichever party was in power.

A symbol of the Prime Minister's own scepticism about educating the electorate in the problems to come was hit direct intervention in the plans to circulate a booklet on social policy at home to troops serving in the Far East. In November 1944 he had authorized the preparation of such a booklet, but when it had been prepared he forbade its circulation until he gave directions.[23] Civil servants even asked his private secretary to secure permission to go ahead while the Prime Minister was at the Potsdam Conference just before the results of the General Election were announced. The troops in the field were never informed as to what the coalition had agreed.

Chapter six
Diplomacy

Churchill was attracted by the idea that the principle of Allied 'combined boards' which had proved successful in strategic planning and war production could also be applied to the field of foreign policy. His regular meetings with Roosevelt and his faith in Anglo-American understanding tempted him into conducting diplomacy at the level of heads of government, in concert with the Americans. He wanted to establish an international order after the war in which Britain and the United States were the dominant alliance of 'English-speaking peoples'. Until the Teheran conference of November 1943, he felt confident of the future. He later confessed that at Teheran he was compelled to face the prospect of an order in which the United States and Russia would make the most important agreements. This turning point in diplomatic relationships coincided with the switch of emphasis in domestic politics towards reconstruction questions.

The rest of the War Cabinet were much more sceptical of the advantages to be gained from the American alliance. Eden who was Foreign Secretary from December 1940 onwards shared the beliefs of his principal Foreign Office advisers who were inclined to hope for some national autonomy in foreign affairs and to proceed with a little bluffing which might disguise the inevitable economic weaknesses of British post-war trade. Eden had on occasion to try to restrain Churchill's enthusiasm for working with the Americans. He was helped in this by Labour members of the coalition, particularly Attlee and Bevin, who were anxious to avoid placing Britain too firmly in an 'English-speaking' alliance. Attlee's ministerial responsibilities at the Dominions Office from February 1942 to September 1943 also provided a Labour Party presence in Cabinet committees on foreign policy. The overseas departments—the Foreign Office, the Colonial Office, and the India Office—were all allocated by Churchill to Conservative ministers. But Eden after November 1942 combined the posts of Foreign Secretary and Leader of the House of Commons. As Leader he had regular contacts with Labour ministers and could easily consult them on foreign policy.

Ironically, the old-fashioned nationalism of Labour ministers in international affairs helped to hold the coalition together when differences within the Cabinet on domestic issues were likely to break it apart. Attlee, who as chairman of the Armistice and Post-War Committee of Cabinet was in touch with the post-hostilities planning arrangements of the Chiefs of Staff, thought that Labour ministers had a duty to see Britain through the awkward transition from war to peace and to avoid any political divisions which would damage the country's standing at international meetings. Both he and Bevin as members of the Defence Committee were fully appraised of the absence of agreement among the Allies on many fundamental questions. They were in a good position to see how little was being achieved by diplomacy and how much was going to depend on the final deployment of armies in the field.

The alliance with the Americans was not in fact as conducive to finding agreement on foreign policy questions as Churchill's contacts with Roosevelt might have led him to suppose. At levels lower than that of the heads of government the differences between the American and the British systems of government were exposed. Roosevelt quite deliberately conducted his own foreign policy with the the loosest form of co-ordination between different departments of state. He could quite easily discount the views of his official advisers, and play off one set of officials against another. American officials were accustomed to compete for Presidential attention, and to recognize the risks of defeat for the policy of particular agencies. Churchill for all his predominance over other members of the Cabinet was constrained to work within the tighter system of co-ordination to which British officials had been trained. He was perhaps inclined to place much too great a faith in his own ability to sort out a problem at the Presidential level, without realizing how much damage had been done to both his own Ministers and senior officials by the frustrations of negotiating with American agencies which were themselves unable to get their own positions accepted in Washington. Whitehall was so familiar with the need to reach interdepartmental agreements before facing the foreign negotiator that the British 'official mind' found it hard to conceive of alternative behaviour. A carefully constructed British reply to American demands which had passed through all the different stages of interdepartmental discussion might well not even be forwarded to other agencies by the American authority involved. The American and British governments did not share a common diplomatic style.

In fact, the insistence of Americans at all levels from the President downwards on getting Britain to reconsider both her position as a colonial power and her policies on international trade injected divisions into the coalition which reduced any likelihood of Anglo-American understanding. The Americans were sufficiently suspicious of British inclinations towards protectionism for the Empire to make bilateral talks on a number of related topics a necessary condition for the granting of aid. Article VII of the Mutual Aid Agreement in March 1942 provided for discussions on international trade, and the American State Department came forward with the idea that the colonial powers should consider a declaration of intent about the future of colonial possessions. In both these fields ministers in the coalition held different opinions, and individual government departments mounted at official level rearguard defences of the interests which seemed to be at risk.

The latent antagonisms between the United Stated and Britain were compounded by the entry of Russia into the concert of powers against Germany, and by the uncertain status enjoyed by the representatives of France in that concert. Whatever might have become the principal areas of agreement between American and British representatives, the Soviet Union was increasingly placed in the position of being able to handicap British ambitions, firstly in 1943 by playing them off against those of the Americans and secondly in 1944 by giving special attention to Free French suspicions about the importance of Britain. The British Cabinet had been thrown into great confusion in December 1941 when Stalin had insisted on a commitment from the British that—with the exception of Poland which would be handled separately—Russia should be allowed to retain the frontiers she had secured in 1940 in the Baltic and in Rumania by force of arms when in alliance with Germany.

The presence of the Free French in London was a constant source of friction between American and British negotiators. It also reminded ministers in the coalition of both Churchill's predilections for special diplomatic relations at the level of heads of government—London was full of European governments in exile—and his supreme determination to fight in 1940 and to avoid the humiliation of the Vichy regime. The drama of the fall of France had given Churchill a special role in diplomacy which he was reluctant to abandon, however pressing his other responsibilities. Desmond Morton as Churchill's personal liaison officer with the Free French embodied diplomatic additions to the Prime Minister's private office which were then extended to cover other 'governments in exile'. Churchill's unstinted support for the declaration of union between Britain and France as the French armies retreated and his dispatch of Lord Lloyd to Bordeaux in a final bid to rally the French against surrender were parts of the aggressive stance which he had built up in the coalition against Chamberlainite inclinations towards appeasement.

The first few months of the coalition had been dominated by the French collapse and by Halifax as Foreign Secretary making proposals in favour of entreating the Germans for peace. The recollection that the War Cabinet under Churchill had in fact contemplated surrender was by 1942 not surprisingly suppressed. The great majority of ministers had supported Churchill's bellicose stand, but the coalition had gradually to be purged of its more diffident elements. Churchill's decision to send Halifax as Ambassador to Washington and to replace him as Foreign Secretary with Eden was a major step in raising the spirits of the Government. Eden at the Foreign Office was 'a man going home'. American negotiators could never quite appreciate the legacy of the fall of France in British susceptibilities.

The success of Eden's diplomacy was qualified under the conditions imposed by Roosevelt's change of front. The President of the United States, who always had a profound distaste for De Gaulle and therefore for the claims of the French which he embodied, came during the course of 1943 to reassess his view of Stalin. Roosevelt saw ways of extending support for his ideas of world organization from the Anglo-American 'Big 2' to an American, Russian and British 'Big 3', and even a 'Big 4' including China. In January 1943 he met Churchill at Casablanca, and in November 1943 he met Stalin and Churchill in Teheran, with preliminary and subsequent discussions in Cairo where Chiang Kai-Shek on behalf of China received assurances that all her territories lost to Japan would be restored. The Moscow declaration of October 1943 committed the 'Big 4' to 'joint actions on behalf of the community of nations', and set in motion the preliminary planning for the creation of the United Nations.

The representatives of the Free French were excluded from both this declaration and the simultaneous creation of the European Advisory Commission, bringing together representatives of the 'Big 3' to plan the post-war organization of Germany as well as the treatment of Austria and other questions affecting the proposed Allied invasion of the Continent. Eden succeeded in getting the Commission to set up its headquarters in London, where the Foreign Office and the British representative could exercise an important influence.

The whole exercise of European reconstruction was dominated by Roosevelt's espousal of the doctrine of unconditional surrender, a view which seems to have come to him after contemplating the difficulties of finding an appropriate authority to represent the defeated and half-occupied France. It seemed better to avoid treating with any enemy government than to face doubts about the legitimacy of what survived. Roosevelt in January 1943 without consulting his allies made a public announcement of this policy at a press conference. Neither Churchill nor his War Cabinet was entirely happy with the doctrine, and the British Chiefs of Staff feared that its public promulgation would only serve to stiffen enemy resistance. British foreign policy was therefore dominated in one major aspect by a declaration on which the British Cabinet had had no real discussions.

The diplomatic problems of the coalition arose largely in the context of Roosevelt's conviction that he could manage Stalin, or at least that there were strong material reasons why he should establish more friendly relations with Stalin when it became clear that Russia would be in a dominant position in Europe after the defeat of Germany. During 1943 Roosevelt began to tire of Churchill's tremendous energy and became more doubtful about the political implications of what he proposed. Churchill was at the same time making a conscious bid to promote an 'English-speaking alliance'. At a lunch in Washington with American dignitaries in May 1943, Churchill had broached the idea of British and American citizens having a common passport and even some kind of common citizenship; in a speech at Harvard University in September 1943, he had publicly suggested that the two countries should continue joint defence planning after the war. After such demonstrations of his expansive mood, he was naturally somewhat chagrined by the cold treatment he received from Roosevelt in Cairo. He was particularly stung by the President's complaint that Eden had behaved badly in preparing a plan to delay the return to Athens of the King of Greece. 'The President's explosion on the way to the aerodrome', as they both left Cairo in December 1943, symbolized an American demotion of British standing and marked the beginning of greater American-Russian agreements. Churchill never fully recovered his position in the 'Big 3', and the 'Big 2' came to mean a partnership from which Britain was excluded.

Another symbol of the switch in Roosevelt's priorities was the re-posting of his personal adviser, Averell Harriman, from London to Moscow. Harriman who had been sent to Britain as the President's special representative was appointed American Ambassador to Russia in 1943. It is hard to estimate how far Roosevelt was by this time beginning to be influenced by the potential diplomatic value which he saw in the possession of the atomic bomb. He appears to have rejected the idea of an Anglo-American monopoly in bomb production and wanted Russia to share in an international arrangement.

Other members of the War Cabinet were not as abashed as Churchill by these symbols of a decline in British power. They often thought he had moved too far in the direction of pleasing Roosevelt. Eden was himself quite happy to see the collapse of some of Churchill's more extravagant plans. For the government as a whole, what mattered was the preservation of British influence in a number of key areas of discussion as the war moved into its final stages.

But there were no diplomatic achievements to hold the coalition together. Neither Churchill nor Eden got his way. The coalition fell without any prospect of a major 'English-speaking alliance' and without any opportunity to acquire sufficient strength for an independent foreign policy. It was remarkable that the machine of war forged ahead without any diplomatic preparation on fundamentals. The American and British armies landed in France on D-Day, 6 June 1944, before the Allies reached agreement on the final form of civilian administration to take over the government of the areas which they were liberating. The 'Big 4' went ahead with the setting up of the United Nations before there was any agreement between the United States and the colonial powers on the future of the colonial peoples. The armies of the 'Big 3' began invading Germany with only the semblance of an agreement on its division into 'zones' for the Allies to occupy. The German government ceased to have any territory to administer, and Doenitz as Hitler's successor was told by the Allies to give up the last vestiges of sovereignty. The issue of zone administration was reopened just as the coalition was being wound up. The major decisions on reconstruction were taken in negotiations at which Britain was represented by Attlee and Bevin as the ministers of a Labour government.

The tensions within the War Cabinet provoked by Churchill's faith in Anglo-American understanding could not be resolved by appeals to public opinion or even intelligent debate in informed circles outside government. Ministers and officials were constrained by the limited opportunities which the war had imposed on cultivating assessments of foreign policy problems in public. Relations with the United States were portrayed in a hazy glow of propaganda, and relations with the Soviet Union were punctuated by campaigns in favour of the 'Second Front' or by maverick publicity stunts run by Lord Beaverbrook. Churchill in these conditions saw opportunities where he might lead opinion; Roosevelt by contrast was very sensitive to the natural caution of Americans towards projects in world affairs. It was precisely on this sense of waiting upon the climate of opinion in Congress that the fate of so many British plans seemed to rest.

Working with the Americans

The temptation to rely on the alliance with the United States was not evenly experienced throughout the government, and the prospect of a joint diplomatic approach on all major issues exposed the latent differences within each political party and between the major departments of state. Working with the Americans revived within the Cabinet many traditional arguments about the choice between free trade and protection, and led the Foreign Office to get embroiled not only in disputes with the other overseas departments but also in disagreements with the Treasury and the Board of Trade which had direct interests in what the Americans were proposing. The coalition was not capable of holding together firmly enough to drive a hard diplomatic bargain in conditions of extreme economic dependence.

It never succeeded in reaching agreement on the two most important issues which arose within the alliance—how to handle the huge debts incurred by the government in the purchase of war supplies and how to secure an appropriate level of American aid to Britain for the indefinite period of transition from war to peace. These issues which were on the agenda of the Cabinet throughout the war could not be resolved without making its disagreements public, an almost impossible condition while the intimacy of the alliance in strategic affairs lasted. The government therefore went through the war acceding to a large number of joint declarations about the future of the United Nations and its proposed agencies but delaying any decision on the crucial factors which were going to determine Britain's position in world affairs. British officials made major contributions to the conferences called to design the different agencies of international co-operation, such as FAO and UNRRA, and acquitted themselves well at Bretton Woods in 1944 when the outlines of the post-war international monetary system were agreed, but they met constant frustration in all the discussions on the future of Britain as a trading nation. When the war came to an end, the Labour government had quickly to reach agreement with the Americans for a loan to Britain against this background of the coalition's delay. Even then the Treasury laid extremely elaborate plans for a period of post-war austerity in case the American Congress did not approve of the agreement.

The coalition's difficulty was apparent long before the United States became a belligerent. The British government thought that the principle of lend-lease, which Roosevelt had promoted in the winter of 1940-41 in order to help the supply of materials to Britain, would place the conduct of its external economic policy largely in

American hands. Not surprisingly, the government resisted falling too deeply into this trap. It looked as if the Americans had the power to determine which goods British industry could export and what level the nation's reserves night be.

Between the Congressional approval of lend-lease and the British government's acceptance of the Mutual Aid Agreement were what Dean Acheson called eleven months of 'blindman's buff'. The American government did not withhold lend-lease during this period, but insisted that when the debts came finally to be settled at the end of the war there would be some specific 'benefit' to the United States—what became known as 'the consideration'. British negotiators anticipating that the country's balance of payments would be in a parlous condition wanted to retain their own forms of control over trade for the first five or six years of peace-time production. It was at this stage of the negotiations that Keynes launched his plan for an International Commercial Union which was later modified to create the International Monetary Fund. It was also at this time that the Treasury found itself at loggerheads with the Foreign Office over the proposed reform of the Diplomatic Service. When the Atlantic Charter was signed by Roosevelt and Churchill in August 1941, Britain avoided any form of words which might compromise its position on trade policy.

But the American government secured the greater part of its conditions when the Mutual Aid Agreement was announced in March 1942. Article VII of that agreement committed Britain to a joint exploration of the international trading system, which meant that the future of imperial preference was brought into question. The Cabinet's agreement to American ideas in February 1942 came after a short period of intense diplomatic activity following Pearl Harbour and the entry of the United States into the war. The argument that Pearl Harbour had wiped out any reference to 'the consideration' was discounted because it might be interpreted as an unfair exploitation of American isolationism. The Cabinet came to the conclusion that it was wiser to reach agreement then. The decision was in part a product of the hope that 'reverse lend-lease' would be introduced and in part a reaction against the previous prevarications.

But the gap between the agreement and the will to implement it by entering into further negotiations was very wide. Churchill, himself at heart a free trader, was not inclined to give the question of talks on trade any priority. Perhaps unconsciously he tended to play down any question on which the American administration felt strongly if it was likely to endanger the internal workings of his own government. The question of abandoning such elements as still remained of imperial preference policy threatened to open up disagreement in the Conservative Party and to lead such ministers as Amery and Beaverbrook into major campaigns of intrigue and obstruction. The danger of opening up divisions between ministers meant that officials were obliged to work at a series of inter-departmental analyses which could not easily find the appropriate ministerial agenda. While the negotiations on 'the consideration' were being conducted in 1941-2, the permanent secretaries of the principal departments of state were meeting regularly in the official committee on internal economic problems. It was in the context of these meetings that some of the major questions were first raised, such as the planning and timing of investment for post-war industry, and that the embarrassment of ministerial differences was first acknowledged.

The preparation of the British position on a number of post-war questions in aid and trade was therefore largely left to the initiative of officials and to the special flavour of enterprise which Dalton encouraged at the Board of Trade. Dalton who became the minister in that department in February 1942 secured the services of Leisching, a senior civil servant from the Dominions Office, to take charge of his commercial policy. James Meade as one of the department's economic advisers promoted a plan for an 'international commercial union' with the help of Hugh Gaitskell. The department sponsored a committee under its permanent secretary to work out with the Treasury and other interested parties all the implications of approaching the Americans to discuss a system of multilateral trade. By the spring of 1943 the British position had been well prepared.

Formal talks with the Americans did not get under way until a mission led by the junior minister at the Foreign Office, Richard Law, visited Washington in September-October 1943. There were technically five main groups of discussions falling within the scope of Article VII of the Mutual Aid Agreement—money, commerce, commodity agreements, cartels and employment. In them, at any rate, the principal British interest lay in getting some form of agreement which would help domestic provisions for employment through international co-operation. Officials were concerned to point out the siginificance of arrangements for money, commerce and commodities in managing to avoid a post-war depression in the economy. But in practice discussions on cartels and employment never made progress. Although the discussions on commodities got entangled with those on the provision of surplus crops for relief and rehabilitation, they resulted in the creation of the Food and Agriculture Organization. In spite of disagreements about the means of stabilizing currencies, the discussions on money led to the establishment of the International Monetary Fund. But there was no basis for a parallel agreement on a 'commercial union'. The Cabinet committee on external economic policy chaired by Anderson after the return of Law's mission from the United States received a minority report in February 1944 from Beaverbrook who wanted a new plan to embrace the sterling area.

The shadow of the unresolved issue of a 'consideration' coloured the coalition's handling of other issues which endangered the unity of the Cabinet. Its influence was particularly apparent in the other major field of policy where American pressure was applied — the future of the colonial peoples. Law had also been chairman of another Cabinet committee which was set up in December 1942 to study the state of American opinion about the British Empire and to propose ways of 'moderating hostile feeling with a view to securing a general sentiment sympathetic to the maintenance of the British imperial system'. The committee was supposed to find means of demonstrating to the United States that the Empire was 'a suitable partner in world affairs', but in fact it succeeded primarily in showing what a wide spectrum of opinion existed inside the coalition. Labour ministers were sympathetic to the proposal that the colonies should be prepared for independence under some kind of international supervision; Churchill and Amery were primarily concerned to restore the *status quo ante bellum*. By the end of 1942 there was considerable resentment against what appeared to be American firms under contract to the United States government taking advantage, for private commercial gain, of the entry into British territories which their special war-time status had given them. British ministers interpreted the speeches and writings of Wendell Wilkie, Roosevelt's Republican opponent, as subtle forms of economic imperialism.

Another area in which the Cabinet was reduced to endless bickering and dispute was the formulation of a policy for civil aviation. It looked as if the war production agreement with the Americans which confined the British airframe industry to constructing fighters and lighter aeroplanes had given the United States the incomparable advantage of having bombers and transports which could easily be converted for civil purposes. Both governments agreed that any post-war settlement should include arrangements both for air traffic control and for licensing air carriers. The overflying rights of some important areas fell under British control, but the ambitions of some British ministers, such as Beaverbrook, to sponsor an 'all-Red Route' round the world by using the British Empire were frustrated by American influence both in Canada and in Australasia. South Africa was in addition anxious to establish its superiority over African air space. As in the discussion of colonial policy, the advocates of the internationalization of civil air transport, particularly on major trunk routes, found little support in the face of the strong expressions of national interest.

During the two years of delay in reaching any satisfactory accord on such a range of important subjects (spring 1942- spring 1944) the scale of British future post-war difficulties became even more apparent to both sides. The immense power of the United States was an almost tangible presence in all-British internal consultations. At the heart of the disagreement was a difference of time scale. The British felt that the Americans were always prone to under-estimate the time required to return the national economy to peace-time conditions. A year for the 'transition' was not unrealistic in the United States, but it was a totally unacceptable estimate in the United Kingdom. At the same time the American government was already preparing for the next Presidential election due in November 1944, while the British government could not even contemplate a General Election before the defeat of Germany.

The Americans were also considering various ways of using British post-war requirements in lend-lease as a means of exercising leverage over the British government in other spheres of policy. There seems little doubt that at the second Quebec Conference in October 1944, Churchill to some extent traded his lend-lease requirements for British agreement to the plans put forward by the Americans in favour of the 'deindustrialization' of Germany—the elimination of the productive capacity of the Ruhr and the Saar—which some called 'pastoralization'—a return to agriculture and stock breeding. In fact, neither the lend-lease requirements nor the 'deindustrial-ization' policy were subsequently implemented. But the barter was itself symbolic of the different standing of the two powers.

Also in the summer of 1944 a number of senior ministers resented the continuous American pressure for Britain to make concessions both on oil production in the Middle East and on the international management of civil aviation. The Allies had established a number of oil refuelling depots for ships and aircraft, and both powers recognized that these would transform post-war communications. It became a matter of common concern to determine which commercial interests might come to use them. The United States, which wanted oil rights in the Middle East, signed a provisional agreement with Britain in August 1944. The preparations for a conference on international air transport, begun in the summer of 1943, were postponed partly by the Presidential election campaign. Informal talks were held in Britain in April 1944 but the full conference did not get under way until October and November. But the British Cabinet had been in considerable disarray before then. The Air Ministry had fought a long rearguard action against the creation of a separate Ministry of Civil Aviation, and the Cabinet had been divided on the extent to which carriers for licensed air routes were to be in the hands of private companies, not BOAC. The latter had been damaged by the creation of RAF Transport Command. The climate of debate was not conducive to finding an agreement with the Americans on war debts, trade and aid.

After the Four Power Declaration in Moscow and the Teheran Conference in October and November 1943, the whole conduct of Allied diplomacy had revolved around geopolitical questions on which Roosevelt had strong personal views and about which the United States could exercise its massive strength. Whatever the theory of combined planning for strategic operations, by 1944 it was clear that the practice of Anglo-American military co-operation had begun to reflect the bias of the American chiefs of staff in favour of the Pacific theatre of war. The doctrine of Germany first, a distasteful idea to many Republicans and former isolationists, was of course fully implemented by the D-Day landings in France, but the Americans had not calculated on the same scope for subsequent joint operations in the Pacific, because Britain just did not have the resources to fight on a number of different fronts with equal effectiveness.[1] The American Navy was in any case jealous to guard its supremacy in the Pacific. The boundaries of the new command in South East Asia under the jurisdiction of the Combined Chiefs were the subject of protracted negotiation between the Americans and British before, during and after the first Quebec Conference in August 1943. The definition of the area in which British military participation was acceptable to American strategic planners was affected by the political role which they envisaged for China in the future. Mountbatten's South East Asia Command was circumscribed by the American strategic doctrine that China provided the decisive base from which to defeat Japan.

While each of the belligerents was anxious to limit his deployment of troops and material, no one wanted a 'Second Front now' if it could be avoided; only the United States could summon up the necessary equipment to manage a 'world war'. Stalin protected himself from attack in the East by signing a neutrality pact with Japan in 1941; Churchill resisted mounting any full-scale invasion of France in 1942-3 while British forces were fully stretched in the eastern Mediterranean; but Roosevelt by 1943 could tolerate the prospect of a 'leakage' of American resources towards the fight against Japan. It was after all true that the American public had a much greater enmity towards the Japanese than towards the Germans, while British public opinion was largely focused upon the menace of Hitler in Europe. With the collapse of British power in the Far East after the fall of Singapore, all the dilemmas confronting British policy-makers came flooding into official discussions as the tensions between creating European order and managing Commonwealth co-operation made themselves felt. Roosevelt's grasp of geopolitics exposed in an acute form the extent of British weakness as both a European and an imperial power.

There were several different levels of understanding inside the coalition about the consequences of American predominance, just as there were differences of emphasis within the conduct of the Anglo-American diplomatic alliance itself. Part of the difficulty for British ministers in assessing what position they should take on American diplomatic moves was not just the confusion they saw in the Washington bureaucracy, but also the doubts which they increasingly entertained about Soviet intentions. Labour ministers had been divided in 1941-2 at the time of the discussion of Stalin's claim to keep his 1941 frontiers. Dalton and Cripps had been more sympathetic to Soviet ambitions than Attlee and Bevin. But all parties in the coalition were driven to protest against the Soviet treatment of Poland at the time of the August 1944 uprising in Warsaw. There were two rival bodies of Polish exiles, in Moscow and in London. The British government found Stalin's refusal to help the Warsaw uprising intolerably partisan. Churchill and Eden fought hard at the Yalta Conference in February 1945 to secure Soviet agreement to free elections in Poland and a 'mixed government' of Moscow and London Poles. But the coalition as a whole was extremely vulnerable to lobbying by London Poles who claimed that the United States was prepared to let the Soviet Union escape from any major limitations on its actions. Both Conservative and Labour MPs doubted Russian good faith.

Nor was it easy for British Ministers to build any alternative strategy on an alliance with a liberated and reinvigorated France. Allied relationships with the Free French placed De Gaulle in a position where he could only seek to exploit any differences between the United States, Britain and Russia. The strength of the French Communist Party in French resistance to German occupation gave the Russians an easy means of entering French politics. The French Committee for National Liberation had been formed in June 1943 with De Gaulle and Giraud as its joint leaders. The Soviet Union in the following months had expressed its willingness to recognize the committee as the future representatives of a liberated France, but the United States and Britain hesitated to follow suit. Roosevelt and Churchill both dragged their feet in spite of pressure from their advisers. The deadlock had only been resolved by separate American, British and Soviet statements in August after the Quebec

Conference. Churchill followed Roosevelt in drawing back from recognizing the French Committee as a provisional government, but only in the face of a massive opposition from his Cabinet colleagues.[2] The recognition of De Gaulle's Committee as the provisional government was not made until Roosevelt took the initiative in October 1944. De Gaulle immediately made approaches towards the Soviet Union in order to strengthen his position with the French Communist Party. In spite of British support at the Yalta Conference for the French claim to occupy a 'zone' in Germany, De Gaulle administered a number of snubs to the British. The message in De Gaulle's communications was that only the United States and Russia had the power to determine the political settlement.

The coalition remained exposed to regular American charges that Britain was fighting a much more 'political' war than the Russians. The strategic problems of the Far East could not be solved without effecting the post-war colonial settlement, and the American authorities were determined not be associated with the reinstatement of what they regarded as an illegitimate colonial authority. By 1943-4 each move taken by the British government was liable to be judged in American eyes either by its relationship to the restoration of the Empire east of Suez or by its relevance to British control over the Middle East and Meditterranean. The government lacked sufficient power to take advantage of either Soviet or French suspicions about the United States. Churchill became much less sure of his ground in the conduct of personal diplomacy.

By 1944 the British alliance with the United States was subject to an increasing number of qualifications in day-to-day practice, restraint in confidential exchanges and reticence in discussion. There appears to have been an extension of the habit on each side of marking cables 'for the eyes' of British or of American officials. The Americans temporized to avoid any serious discussion of the proposal that the Combined Chiefs of Staff should be retained after the war was over.

Official British estimates at the end of the war on the aid which the British economy needed from the United States varied between $5 billion and $8 billion. The country's external liabilities were £3,355 million—£2,723 million owed in the sterling area, while its liquid assets were only £453 million. It was calculated that Britain needed to export goods at a rate of between 50 and 75 per cent more than pre-war levels in order to compensate for losing a quarter of her national wealth since 1939 and for the penalties of running a large overseas deficit. The fact that the coalition had failed to reach agreement with the Americans on both British debts and the future shape of world trade was an immense handicap to the incoming Labour government.

Personal diplomacy

By the early months of 1944 even before the coalition had begun to reconsider its own political future, there were already within government a number of raised voices suggesting that Churchill was himself a diplomatic handicap. As his influence on the joint planning of military strategy began to ebb, his critics in foreign policy made themselves heard. It was a year of great strain. The whole war machine had been tuned to full pitch for the invasion of France, and the arrangements for making this effort had deliberately contained provisions to begin switching resources towards peace-time requirements. The planning of war production included in its manpower budgets an anticipation of peace which encouraged more forthright expressions of hope from Ministers and officials alike. Not only were Churchill's personal prejudices now likely to be more abrasive, but also Roosevelt's health gave cause for alarm. Although Roosevelt was set to fight another Presidential election campaign, British observers of the American scene began to doubt whether he had the stamina required and whether he was capable of conducting public affairs. By the time Roosevelt and Churchill met Stalin at Yalta in February 1945, the American President was clearly a very sick man. He died in April. For all the previous year many of Churchill's colleagues had been sceptical of the faith which Churchill had placed in his own relationship with an ailing President. Churchill's predilection for personal diplomacy was seen to be a diminishing asset.

But the first major strictures from Cabinet colleagues against Churchill's personal diplomacy had been made even before the United States entered the war. Article 3 of the Atlantic Charter which Roosevelt and Churchill had signed in August 1941 appeared to apply the principle of self-determination—'the right of all peoples to choose the form of government under which they will live'—to any post-war settlement. Amery as Secretary of State for India was concerned about the effects of the declaration in that sub-continent; Attlee was prepared to see it as a major step forward in colonial policy. The Colonial Office which had already set up a departmental committee to look into colonial service reform was anxious to avoid giving way to American criticisms of the standards of native administration. The Atlantic Charter meeting was but a foretaste of the dangerous commitments which might arise from 'summit' meetings between heads of government. Churchill's agreement then to self-determination was partly a reference to German-occupied Europe, and partly a general stance which was designed to avoid declaring war on Japan by relying on the Chinese to bear the brunt of Japanese aggression. Japan's attack on Pearl Harbour transformed the context of discussion on the future of the colonial empires.

The greatest source of strain in Cabinet on colonial affairs was the decision to treat with nationalist leaders in India in 1942. The presence of Japanese armies in Burma brought pressure on the British government to make some gesture that would retain the loyalty of Indian leaders to the Allied cause. Churchill had for a long time been opposed to any further plans for constitutional reform in the government of India, and privately welcomed the fact that communal conflict between Hindus and Moslems enabled the British authorities to play one against the other. The differences between Churchill and his ministers were exacerbated by Roosevelt's personal intervention. The American President proposed setting up a 'temporary Dominion government', using as his example the articles of confederation drawn up by the original thirteen American colonies. This tactless comparison and the abrasive character of his personal representative, Colonel Johnson, whom he sent to New Delhi, did little to improve his chances of persuading Churchill that concessions were required. Furthermore these criticisms coincided with the attacks being made on Churchill at home for his management of the machinery of strategic planning and war production, and with the divisions in Cabinet over the conditions being attached by Stalin to an Anglo-Russian mutual aid treaty. Although the threat was no more than a bluff, Churchill in April 1942 in fact indicated that he would rather resign as Prime Minister than be driven by Roosevelt into making concessions to the Indians.[3]

What the Cabinet decided was to send Sir Stafford Cripps on a special mission to discuss alternative lines of constitutional advancement with the nationalist leaders. Cripps who spent late March and early April 1942 in India wavered between the caution of the Cabinet committee at home and the excessive demands of the leaders who came to see him. The Hindu leaders were completely out of sympathy with British proposals for a separate Moslem state. It became quickly apparent that there were no grounds for an agreement in India, and even more obviously that the Cabinet was unlikely to resolve its own differences of opinion. Gandhi in India was arrested in August after instigating a civil disobedience movement, and Subhas Chandra Bose went over to the Japanese who supported the Government of 'Free India' in Singapore and his 'Indian National Army'. The series of discussions inside the Cabinet had brought to the forefront of ministerial minds how reactionary and how racially prejudiced Churchill could be. Amery as Secretary of State for India was shocked by the Prime Minister's stubbornness, and Dorman-Smith, a former Conservative minister in Chamberlain's Cabinet who as Governor of Burma had been compelled to retreat by the Japanese advance, found that the Prime Minister was totally unprepared to contemplate any post-war plans for Burmese constitutional development.

The paradox of the coalition's approach to affairs in the Far East was that British policy for the area provoked the greatest American suspicion, while in India or South East Asia Command those concerned with British preparations thought that they faced a relative indifference in London. Visitors to the capital from this theatre of war often complained that they had been forgotten, or that the Foreign Office, Colonial Office, and the service departments were not making sufficient efforts to get ready for the restoration of British imperial power. The Malayan Planning Unit set up in 1943 by the Colonial Office and War Office worked at a fairly junior official level. Many of the earlier arguments that Far Eastern affairs merited their own Secretary of State had largely been forgotten.

American suspicions rested primarily on the apparent British preference for amphibious operations against the islands and peninsulas of South East Asia instead of a land campaign in Burma and China. John Paton Davies, the American Liaison Officer between the United States forces and Chiang Kai-Shek, was still adamant in September 1943 that Britain was planning to prevent China from developing into a major power, and conserving British manpower until it could be used for a repossession of the Empire.[4] This viewpoint encouraged the idea in American official circles that the colonial powers which had lost territory to the Japanese—Britain, France and Holland—were secretly arranging some form of concerted action. Churchill's general attitude and the behaviour of British officers in the field tended to confirm in American minds a number of unworthy stereotypes of imperialism.

The greatest handicap to any improvement in Anglo-American relations on questions east of Suez was the British refusal either to reach agreement with Indian nationalists or to make some kind of declaration on a time-table for granting independence to the colonial peoples. The Department of State in Washington pressed the Colonial Office to consider various ways of issuing a 'Colonial Charter'. This pressure had the embarrassing effect of showing the Colonial Secretary that there was no set of explicit promises on colonial development, only a number of generalizations in which eventual independence was assumed. It also demonstrated that the Americans had no conception of the idea that there was already an established path of constitutional progress through the different stages which led eventually to Dominion status. Throughout 1942-3 various diplomatic exchanges explored the American preference for some kind of international supervision over colonial development. By the spring of 1943 it looked as if the British government was prepared to accept supervision by a series of regional commissions set up by the colonial powers. An important point of agreement in 1942, in spite of considerable official opposition in Whitehall, had been the signing of the articles of co-operation which set up the Anglo-American Commission for the Caribbean.

The strains of Anglo-American co-operation in the Far East also introduced into the War Cabinet some consideration of Churchill's apparent insensitivity to the claims of Dominion governments in the Commonwealth. Australia and New Zealand depended on the presence of American forces in the Pacific for their defence. The loss of Malaya to the Japanese meant that the principal routes for aircraft between London and Australasia were through the United States; the old Imperial Airways-Qantas route through India was closed, and only a very limited service from Africa across the Southern Indian Ocean was permitted, and that relying on the American-built Catalina flying-boat. Canada was always aware that its war production plans had to relate to those of the United States. Curtin, the Prime Minister of Australia, and Mackenzie King, the Prime Minister of Canada, were particularly forceful in expressing their desire to present a special Dominions view within the Anglo-American Alliance.

Both Cranborne and Attlee as Dominion Secretaries were on occasion constrained to remind Churchill of Dominions wishes to be heard. Cranborne in 1941 had made a strong protest against Churchill's conduct of affairs without consulting or even informing the Dominion high commissioners in London of the course of negotiations. The Dominions Secretary liked to work with the High Commissioners whenever he could. They used to have regular 'tea meetings' in the Dominions Office. But Churchill had strong objections to giving the Dominions Prime Ministers a more formal representation in War Cabinet. In 1941 while the threat of attack from Japan seemed imminent, Menzies as Prime Minister of Australia had raised the question of creating an Imperial War Cabinet on a Commonwealth basis. Churchill argued that the presence of Smuts in the Lloyd George coalition in 1917 was not a precedent to be followed. Dominions Prime Ministers were welcome as visitors, as Menzies had been in the spring of 1941, but not as regular attenders. Curtin, Menzies's successor, appointed a special representative in London who had a somewhat awkward role. Curtin also objected to Churchill's selection of R. G. Casey, the Australian minister in Washington, to be the War Cabinet's 'resident minister' in the Middle East.

The only Dominions Prime Minister to enjoy easy access to Churchill was General Smuts, the Prime Minister of South Africa. It is, however, hard to assess his influence on the conduct of affairs. Churchill liked to talk over problems with him when he could, and Smuts paid regular visits to Britain throughout the war, being present, for example, at the final meetings before the D-Day landings in 1944. He attended the diplomatic discussions in Cairo both in 1942 when the strategy of the war in Egypt was discussed, and in 1943 at the time of the 'Big 3' negotiations. His standing was in part derived from South Africa's interest in the supply of arms and men to the Eastern Mediterranean.

In contrast with the position in the Far East, the Cabinet was able to mark out almost a British preserve in the Mediterranean, particularly when the course of the war raised the questions of reconstituting the governments of Italy and Greece. Churchill again indulged himself in a great deal of personal diplomacy, with Eden's support, except when the latter was on sick leave in April 1944. The Cabinet had on several occasions to assert its right to be consulted. So many of the key decisions were taken in direct negotiations between Roosevelt, Churchill and Stalin. Roosevelt had a particular interest in finding an Italian settlement which appealed to the Italian-American voters of the Democratic Party, and tried hard to push the claims of Count Sforza in any Italian provisional government. Stalin was in touch with the Communist Party guerillas in both Greece and Yugoslavia. In October 1944, Churchill on meeting Stalin in Moscow had agreed to divide the Balkans into separate spheres of influence, giving Russia a free hand in Rumania and Britain a predominant influence in Greece. Hungary and Yugoslavia by the same agreement were divided fifty-fifty. Stalin stood by his agreement over Greece, and when the British sent 60,000 troops to help the government in Athens, he made no move to help the Communist partisans.

The Cabinet was much more divided by Churchill's commitments to Greece than by his corresponding set of decisions on Italy, especially when the Greek civil war began in December 1944. But by that date the coalition was obviously not likely to survive the defeat of Germany. Attlee had taken a stand against Churchill in June of that year when Churchill tried to undermine the new Italian government of Senor Bonomi who had replaced Field Marshal Badoglio after the fall of Rome to the Allied armies. After Attlee had reminded the Prime Minister that Cabinet ought to have discussed the messages sent to Roosevelt and Stalin before their despatch, Churchill eventually abandoned his idea of trying to restore Badoglio and supported Roosevelt's declaration in favour of extending governmental responsibility to the Italian people—well timed for the Presidential election campaign. But in the Greek crisis the Prime Minister was not even in tune with his own Foreign Secretary. Eden for more than a year had attempted to persuade Churchill that the only practicable way of setting up a provisional Greek government was to persuade the exiled king that he should give way to a regent, because only by such a move would the guerilla leaders be able to join in and accept responsibility. The resistance was led largely by Communists and followers of Venizelos, who opposed the return of the king. The civil war had begun after the liberation when the British commander in November 1944 asked the guerrilla forces to lay down their arms without giving them any guarantees about their future. The Communist guerilla army had benefited from the accident that nearly all the Italian arms captured at the time of the Italian surrender in August 1943 had fallen into its hands. When the country was divided into Italian, German and Bulgarian zones of occupation, the greater part of the peninsula had been in Italian hands. These guerillas first set up a provisional government inside Greece in March 1944, and then entered into discussions with the government in exile led by Papandreou to form a coalition. Such an organization of national unity entered Athens in October behind the retreating Germans. But in December, perhaps following the example of Tito in Yugoslavia, the Greek Communists left the coalition and showed how easily their forces could dominate the countryside. The War Cabinet during December met a number of times to discuss Greece, but each time Churchill found an excuse for not taking steps to replace the king with the regent. Only a Christmas visit to Athens by Churchill and a reluctant Eden brought the Prime Minister to accept the necessity for a regent and to persuade the king to withdraw.

The public stance taken by the British government on Greece, which looked very much like support for a right-wing government against a popular uprising, came in for much public criticism, especially in the Labour Party at its annual conference in December 1944. Labour ministers were somewhat embarrassed by the delay in reaching a decision. On a motion of censure about Greece in the House of Commons at the beginning of December, only 23 Labour MPs supported the government; the rest either voted against or abstained. The government had got itself embroiled in an almost insoluble political problem and in what looked like an endless civil war.

Attlee was equally embarrassed by the awkward disagreements between the Allies on the proposed administration of an occupied Germany, but he could not voice his misgivings in public. The plan adopted by the European Advisory Commission in March 1944 was confirmed by the 'Big 3' at Yalta in February 1945. This provided for three zones of occupation, Britain in the north-west, America in the south-west, and Russia in the east. Partly because Britain and America still wanted Russian aid against Japan, they did not try to modify the large Russian share. But the zones, although they followed the basic pattern occupied by the invading armies—Britain was on the left wing and America on the right when entering Germany from France—were lines of demarcation once peace was declared, not military objectives. Eisenhower as supreme commander in March 1945 to the horror of the British Cabinet announced to the Russians that he was not driving directly on to Berlin, thus giving them an opportunity to accelerate their advance on the German capital. Until this point, Stalin had deliberately held back from making an attempt to capture Berlin until after his Western allies had crossed the Rhine, in the hope that he could avoid alarming them about his political intentions.

It was precisely on such questions as the position of Russia in a reconstructed Europe that ministers resented the apparent influence on Churchill of his immediate confidants such as Cherwell, Beaverbrook and Bracken. A feature of Churchill's personal diplomacy was that he listened to a lot of informal advice. Eden was particularly annoyed that Cherwell at the second Quebec conference had helped to persuade Churchill that he should accept the proposals of Henry Morgenthau, the Secretary of the United States Treasury, in favour of the 'pastoralization' of Germany which meant the wholesale removal of German heavy industry. Eden succeeded in getting the plan quashed, but not before he had been publicly rebuked by Churchill at the conference and not before Stalin had shown great interest in the prospect of dismantling German production lines for removal to Russia. Beaverbrook was also widely criticized by his minsterial colleagues for interference in matters which should not have concerned him. Some thought him responsible for the various shifts in Churchill's approach towards the Russians. Both Beaverbrook and Bracken, each with close ties in the business of newspapers, prided themselves on their influence over public opinion and formed a kind of alliance within Churchill's most intimate 'secret circle'. They were both at the time of the Warsaw uprising extremely critical of the 'London Poles', and gave support to Stalin's intransigence.

Frustration and delay

The price of Churchill's personal diplomacy and the diminished influence of Britain in the counsels of the 'Big 3' was considerable frustration at the working levels of professional diplomacy. The Foreign Office and the other overseas departments felt the brunt of ministerial disagreements and frequently found themselves with completely abortive plans for the conduct of negotiations. Furthermore officials working closely with senior ministers discovered on occasion that what had apparently been agreed at the level of principal agencies — the Foreign Office and the Department of State for example — was totally overthrown in chance bargains struck between the heads of government. The officials responsible for responding to American requests for a Colonial Charter were never quite sure how far their proposals might be taken in Washington. Nearly all the work on designing 'regional commissions' for co-operation between the colonial powers on economic and social policies was overthrown in the bargaining which took place at Yalta and in the San Francisco conference on the United Nations.

Paradoxically, the major departments of state extended the range of their administrative work to include overseas arrangements but lost the power with which to defend the country's interests. The overseas finance division of the Treasury was expanded to keep pace with the payments problems presented by lend-lease, and Sir Thomas Phillips, the Second Secretary in charge, spent much of his time in Washington — a situation which in 1942 brought in Sir Wilfred Eady as an additional second secretary. Financing war gave the Treasury unique opportunities for administrative specialization. The Board of Trade at the same time increased the scope of its commercial relations department to cover the demands both of talks on Article VII and of consultations with the Dominions. This department became particularly well informed on the state of American opinion: its 'reconstruction' reading lists were full of American references, because so much seemed to depend on what Congress would debate. Even the Colonial Office decided to place an assistant under secretary full-time on overseas questions and international scientific co-operation, and to develop its own 'international relations' department for the run-up to the trusteeship discussions at the San Francisco meeting of the United Nations.

A great deal of what mattered to the maintenance of the Anglo-American alliance did not affect Ministers or even the Prime Minister himself. There was always the much lower-level diplomacy of negotiating strategic and supply questions, and this was conducted in the official committees of mixed committees of Ministers and officials which supported the combined planning operations. The Cabinet came to depend on details being worked out by sub-committees and working parties. Indeed, some committees were primarily important for the secretariats which serviced them. Such secretariats provided a new form of government agency which could easily be adapted to changing circumstances. The Allied Supplies Executive, for example, was a committee established under Beaverbrook in September 1941 to programme supplies to Russia; the North American Supply Committee formed in July 1940 to organize the demands made upon the British Purchasing Mission in Washington was by 1942 largely superseded by its own secretariat, staffed jointly by the Cabinet Office and the Ministry of Production, and then renamed the Joint American Secretariat. Cabinet Office staff in these circumstances were treated as diplomats. On occasions the overseas departments handled subjects which required almost daily consultation through an official Cabinet Committee whose secretariat became the recognized experts in the field. The Committee on Foreign Resistance, begun just after the fall of France under the chairmanship of an official from the Ministry of Economic Warfare, handled many of the delicate questions arising from the division between the Vichy regime and the Free French. It met at least once a week for the first two years of the war, and was serviced by several sub-committees.

Ministers never established a 'foreign policy committee' of Cabinet. Churchill's regular journeys around the world for meetings of heads of government encouraged him either to consult the War Cabinet by telegram or to try out ideas on a single minister alone, particularly Attlee, who could indicate the general feelings of Labour Ministers. Eden when he was anxious to modify some of Churchill's commitments tended to behave in a similar manner. Many major diplomatic questions were discussed in this *ad hoc* way. Cabinet did, however, take special steps to set up ministerial committees if there were subjects which needed special attention. Churchill himself insisted on chairing the Cabinet Committee on India in 1942 at the time of the Cripps Mission; Herbert Morrison was invited to chair the Committee on Palestine in 1943 and 1944, one of the few occasions on which a Labour Minister was permitted a leading role in foreign policy. Attlee chaired the small committee on Malaya and Borneo in 1944, but in general his tenure in 1942-3 of the post of Dominions Secretary did not carry with it a large number of chairmanships. Cranborne, his predecessor and successor at the Dominions Office, carried weight with Churchill and chaired the Cabinet Committee which prepared for the meeting of Dominions Prime Ministers in 1944.

The nearest thing to a general 'foreign policy committee' was the Armistice and Post-War Committee of which Attlee was the chairman. This was originally created in August 1943 to deal with all the many intractable problems arising from the 'civil administration' of territories which the Allies either liberated or occupied. It monitored the Joint Anglo-American Combined Civil Affairs Committee in Washington and tried to disentangle the conflicting claims of commodity policy, relief policy and military administration when the Board of Trade and the War Office were at cross purposes. The War Office in 1941 had originally been given responsibility for 'civil administration' planning. But with the prospect of the Dominion Prime Ministers' meeting, this committee was asked to extend itself to cover a number of political and military questions, including the 'zoning' of occupied Germany and the Dumbarton Oaks meeting to create the United Nations. By the summer of 1944, Attlee was presiding over the work prepared by the Foreign Office relief department and the control commissions for Germany and Austria, and was in regular consultation with both the chiefs of staff for post-hostilities planning and the Ministry of Production for supplies. The expansion of the concept of 'civil administration' gave Attlee a better apprenticeship in foreign policy than his Dominions Office experience.

But the disposition of offices and chairmanships between Ministers left little opportunity to bring together the foreign and domestic aspects of Britain's own post-war reconstruction in a manner comparable to that applied when discussing the same subjects in Europe. The plans for governing an occupied Germany were naturally prepared by relating the administrative apparatus which the Allies were providing to the policies which they agreed to apply in order to restore the German economy. Each step in this process of designing 'civil administration' with its special emphasis on the 'de-nazification' of the German people—the removal of all the symbols of Hitler's power—meant taking account of what aid could be given from outside. The question of asking the Germans to make reparations, to compensate for their deliberate reduction of the industrial potential of those countries which they had occupied, was balanced against the question of supplying German civilians with sufficient food and clothes to see them through the aftermath of invasion and destruction. Britain as one of the victors could not make a similar set of calculations to tide it over its own 'transition'.

The tragedy of the tensions in Cabinet between the strategy of building on an 'English-speaking alliance' and the hopes for a more autonomous existence was that British reconstruction planning was always waiting upon what the American government might do for domestic reasons. Just as Roosevelt had frequently been tempted to interfere in general reviews of post-war reconstruction whenever his political support in the United States needed strengthening, so all American negotiators at lower levels came to look over their shoulders at what they saw as the influence of public opinion. Churchill was never so close as Roosevelt to the immediate demands of domestic politics, nor his ministers as anxious as American bureau chiefs to listen to lobby representatives. Churchill's espousal of greater co-operation with the Americans was a constant reminder of the fact that Roosevelt did not manage a coalition, but a partisan administration which had many committed opponents. Washington officials could never afford to ignore what Congress might do.

The heart of Britain's diplomatic weakness was the danger that the American government might take action against British industry in order to protect the level of employment in the United States. British officials in their dealings with American counterparts were acutely sensitive to the risks of provoking action in line with traditional American isolationism and protectionism. It was painful to face the prospect of immense war debts and of balance of payments difficulties without some hope of American aid. Treasury and Board of Trade officials in the intermittent discussions of 1943-4 seem to have been hoping that at the end of the war Britain could secure some kind of 'grand accommodation' which would provide the necessary support as either a gift or a loan with a low rate of interest. But they at the same time feared that they might themselves have to instigate discriminatory practices against American industrialists in order to prevent the British home market being swamped with consumer goods. The unspoken assumptions of diplomatic preparations for the peace were that import controls would be imposed and that exports would be promoted in the most active manner possible. The employment policies of the two Allied governments might well be incompatible.

Conclusion

The Churchill coalition was a unique combination of ministers brought together by a House of Commons anxious for a special regime that would ensure national survival in total war. Churchill himself did not impose a general acceptance of the doctrine that the war was total and the enemy uncompromising; he came to power to give expression to what MPs already felt about the nature of the struggle which the country faced. They had had plenty of time to consider the price to be paid. The period which became known as 'the phoney war'—September 1939 to April 1940—was an opportunity for reflection on the previous two years of diplomatic activity and for initiation into the anticipated horrors of aerial bombardment. It was not until April 1940 that the first British civilian was killed on British soil by a German air attack—a road-mender in the Orkneys—and that the Germans showed their potential by seizing the principal ports in Norway. But the new government which Churchill formed in May inherited a store of nationalist feeling on which it could capitalize. The House of Commons caught the mood of the people.

It has always been difficult in retrospect to describe the character of the regime which was then created. The task of reconstructing what the coalition was like requires something more than a biography of Churchill, and an account of events more uniquely British—or as would probably have then been said, 'more English'—than that which emerges naturally from an attempt to describe the conduct of the battle. It is not sufficient to understand the psychology of Churchill, or to appreciate the crucial factors which enabled the Allies to defeat the Axis. Any exploration into the nature of this government requires a feel for the insularity of the British political tradition within Europe, a sense of what then constituted the national identity, and a sympathy for the cleansing effects of war on the intellectual disputes of the 1930s. This book is designed to be no more than a beginner's guide to the explorer's requirements.

But it still remains hard to get behind the consequences of

victory and the euphoria of the Labour Party after the General Election of 1945. Just as men of letters quickly built up a myth about the intellectual errors of the 1930s—Malcolm Muggeridge wrote *The Thirties* during the 'phoney war'—so politicians and officials also clothed the ineptitudes of war management with a myth of consensus and good morale. The year in which the country stood 'alone' from June 1940 to June 1941 was both a testing time for national identity and an opportunity to improvise with whatever came to hand in both resources and organization. It seems likely that there will always be many unanswered questions about the effects of war on political thinking and action.

Contemporaries who resented the rapid creation of a national mythology found themselves extremely inhibited in what they could publish or broadcast. The almost tangible mood of a national resolve to fight followed quickly on the heels of support for appeasement. Basil Liddell Hart, for example, who had enjoyed such a universal pre-war reputation for his teaching of the strategy of 'the indirect approach' found that *The Times* refused to take his articles. His criticisms of the doctrine of total war and his demonstrations of the vain pursuit of victory went largely unheard. Few listened to his arguments in favour of conciliation and a negotiated settlement with the Germans.[1] His contention that the introduction of conscription was a major threat to freedom seemed to those who discussed the subject with him almost unworthy of comment. It was already too late in their eyes to count the long-term costs of sacrifice. The 'year alone' meant short-term calculations in a strategy of survival. There seemed to be no virtue in relying on conciliation if there were no prospect of finding the means to compel the German government to keep an agreement. Although the Churchill Cabinet initially contained some ministers, such as Halifax, who hoped for a negotiated peace, the coalition inherited an acceptance of total war.

The principal interest to contemporaries and to many people since has been to try to calculate what modifications in the conventions of political life were introduced by these short-term calculations. The price of improvisation might have been a permanent charge. It has also been important to see whether a new class of people entered public life through the exigencies of the moment. The acceptance of total war meant by definition massive civilian involvement in the battle. It also seemed to bring into prominence a range of talents which had hitherto not been deployed in government service, or at least only consulted intermittently. The engines of war recruited the accumulated experience of the pre-war generation, particularly in science, mathematics, engineering and ecology.

The people whose latent talents were revealed under the aegis of the coalition were not the propagandists in the fight against fascism, but the hard-headed experimentalists of the research laboratories. It was more valuable to the war effort to have joined the Clarendon Laboratory in Oxford in the late 1920s or early 1930s than to have contributed to *Oxford Poetry* or *New Signatures,* the collections which shaped the 'moral landscape' of the pre-war literary world. The skills which produced the creative streak in British strategy and economy of effort came from the excitement of being in Cambridge during the late 1920s rather than from the routines of the Committee of Imperial Defence. As Samuel Hynes has pointed out, 'for the writers *as writers,* the appropriate response to the end of the thirties was silence... it was not really their war... it came not as a cause, but as a consequence of a cause that had already been lost.'[2] It is perhaps dangerous to generalize. So many strands in British intellectual life were woven in new patterns by the need to recruit appropriate personnel to manage the mobilization of the economy, or perhaps more accurately, by the reckless and haphazard exercises in self-promotion and clique creation which the emergency permitted. Goronwy Rees described his visits to Guy Burgess's flat in London as 'rather like watching a French farce which had been injected with all the elements of political drama.'[3] This metaphor which he thought appropriate to a collection of temporary civil servants and girl secretaries, including Communists or ex-Communists, all gossiping about the progress of the war and the conduct of the political machine, conveys the flavour of the energies released by the national crisis.

The coalition came into existence without threatening the grass-roots support of each political party or breaking the principal loyalties between party leaders. The Conservative Party, although it did not immediately come to terms with Churchill as its leader rather than Chamberlain, was not ridden with the sharp antagonisms which split the Liberal Party between Lloyd George and Asquith in 1915-16. The origins of the coalition allowed Churchill to encompass without any apparent signs of incongruity both a sense of enormous personal power and a remarkable respect for the traditions of accountability to the House of Commons. He referred to the House as 'the foundation of the British life struggle'.[4]

The coalition also inherited the sense of trust among politicans of all parties which enabled the House of Commons to go into 'secret session' whenever security considerations demanded a restriction on public debate. Even William Gallagher as the sole Communist MP, under suspicion while Nazi Germany and Soviet

Russia were joined in a non-agression pact, was inclined to thank his colleagues for the forbearance they had shown. MPs were subsequently proud of the freedom of discussion which secret sessions had given them.

Parliament protected itself from surprise attack by not making public its hours and dates of meeting. The bombs which fell on the House of Commons and destroyed the chamber on 10 May 1941 were an accident which did not deter its members. Twenty-eight of the secret sessions dealt with the air raid precaution arrangements of hours and times of meeting; thirty-seven sessions in all were held in order to debate major questions of strategy and security.[5] There is no record of what was said, but those debates became a regular feature of parliamentary life, whereas during the First World War only three secret sessions were held. Chamberlain before his resignation had already conceded the principle of secret sessions, although somewhat reluctantly, after agitation by Sinclair, the Liberal Leader, and requests from the Labour opposition; and the first secret debate was on 14 December 1939 to discuss the Ministry of Supply. By the time Churchill came to give his celebrated secret address to the House about the fall of France on 20 June 1940, he was able to take account of a new set of parliamentary conventions.

The other 'self-denying ordinance' was on the allocation of paper and newsprint between the parties. Paper consumption was regulated by order like the majority of scarce raw materials, and users were allowed quantities based on the size of previous purchases. It was some measure of the acceptance by the coalition of a temporary suspension of party rivalry, that paper allocations were not a political issue. It was not until the beginning of 1944 that the Common Wealth Party was able to make a shift in the allocation of paper for party periodicals by claiming that three MPs merited some formal acknowledgement.

Neither Australia nor Canada when faced with the chance of forming a national coalition with this degree of cohesion was able to find a comparable set of formulae. In Australia Menzies resigned as Prime Minister when he failed to get the backing of all parties for a trip to London in August 1941. Fadden formed a coalition but without the Labour Party.[6] The Labour Party then came to power in October 1941 with a parliamentary majority of only two, refusing to contemplate joining the United Australia and United Country Parties in a coalition. In Canada, Mackenzie King as the Liberal Party Prime Minister offered to take members of the opposition parties into his Cabinet in the summer of 1941, soon after a General Election in which his party had won the largest ever majority of seats and the largest ever proportion of the popular vote. But the leaders of all three parties in the opposition declined to be involved even in consultation, advice, and confidential information on the war effort.[7] In both these countries the idea of introducing conscription for military service was highly controversial. In Canada the Conservative Party in opposition pressed the Liberal government to endorse the value of conscription. Indeed, Meighen, the Conservative Party leader, saw the issue of conscription as a means of getting 'into action on strong British total war lines.[8]

The entry of the United States into the war also emphasized the unique character of the British governmental regime. The Americans were always tempted to treat Churchill as if he were a President, when in fact he exercised personal authority with a rather unusual parliamentary sanction. The British for their part were always inclined to forget that Roosevelt as President still faced a partisan opposition to his government, not only in Congress but also in the country at large. There was no American equivalent of 'the electoral truce' which might have softened Republican criticisms of the Democratic President. As the tide of battle flowed strongly against British arms during the first few months after the American entry—with a British retreat in the western desert, massive losses in the Atlantic shipping lanes, and the collapse of the imperial defence system in Malaya and Burma—it became clearer to American commentators that Churchill would lose his parliamentary standing only by military defeat. The coalition was an expression of support for a war leader. Churchill might have been replaced by another war leader with coalition backing, such as Cripps, if the latter had been able to pin the blame for defeat on Churchill's miscalculation; but the government would still have been an expression of national sentiment, not of party calculation.

The reasons why the Churchill coalition began to change its character after the winter of 1942-3 were primarily military. The short-term calculations for national survival were then gradually displaced by longer-term calculations about the consequences of different strategies for a lasting peace. Liddell Hart's arguments on the dubious value of victory and the futility of total war, which had been widely ignored from 1939 to 1942, became slightly more acceptable in 1943. He was not alone in thinking that Roosevelt's declaration of a policy of 'unconditional surrender' in January 1943 was an unmitigated disaster.[9]

The 'turn of the tide' in Allied military success affected every aspect of the coalition's existence. By the time of the second Battle of El Alamein in October 1942 the government had survived almost two and a half years with only minor changes of personnel, and the nation had been equipped for war for over three years. By May 1943, German U-boats had been compelled to withdraw from the greater part of the Atlantic, and by July 1943 the invasion of Italy had driven Mussolini to resignation. The agenda of the Anglo-American conference in Quebec in August 1943 was dominated by considerations of victory and the future world order. Ministers in the coalition could then see how the next stage in planning for war production was to be the winding down of effort after the supreme sacrifice of the invasion of Europe; they could envisage the government finding sufficient common ground to put forward a social policy; and they could begin to anticipate a diplomatic offensive for gaining influence in the proposed United Nations. The political party conferences in May and June 1943 were therefore occasions on which to begin to think the unthink-able—that the coalition might not survive, and that a war leader might be a positive handicap in planning reconstruction.

By the summer of 1943 ministers and officials began to assess the consequences of action which had been taken in each area of government policy to meet the immediate short-term needs of national survival. Those who had accompanied the Prime Minister to Quebec in August were aware on their return home that four years of war might well have created circumstances in which such actions had had unanticipated long-term effects. Above all, everything which Britain had done in the desperation of 1940-41 had been to some extent superseded by the mobilization of the United States economy against the Axis powers. No authority in Britain could prepare for the future outside the terms of the Anglo-American alliance. While the latter induced different sets of hopes among those concerned with the policy for the transition from war to peace, it could not be ignored. Similarly, ministers and officials felt bound to assess the effects of mobilization on society and economy. The debate on the Beveridge Report had brought out a lot of evidence about the extent to which the electorate wanted a degree of social reform. Even the elderly and moderate wing of the Conservative Party had been compelled to recognize that the electors expected to see some kind of 'Welfare State' established at the end of the war. The fourth Marquess of Salisbury who had served in the Cabinets of Balfour and Bonar Law published a pamphlet in 1942 when he was eighty-one in order to affirm his belief that state action and private enterprise were complementary.[10] He admitted that nationalization had its place and that private enterprise should be subject to reasonable guidance by the State.

In making their assessment of what had happened ministers and officials did not normally distinguish between the value of coalition and the effects of mobilization itself. Only in matters affecting the technicalities of replacing emergency regulation by normal peace-time statutory authority was it natural to applaud a non-partisan approach. A coalition of all the major parties could bear the unpopularity of retaining controls without suffering the criticism which a party government would attract. In other fields of policy it was much more difficult to proclaim the advantages of coalition or indeed to ascribe particular consequences to its presence.

Paradoxically the advantages of coalition were more obvious in precisely those fields of activity in which the Churchill government had received the largest inheritance from its predecessor—strategic planning and the mobilization of industry. It was much more difficult to distinguish the precise contribution to the war effort which the all-party administration had brought if the rearmament policy and technical inventions of the late 1930s were recognized to place limits on what battles could be fought, and if the defence contracts of the National Government and the control regulations it had devised were acknowledged to be the basis of managing the economy. In retrospect, even in 1943, the coalition seemed to have been primarily important for giving legitimacy and consent to what was already under way in the preparations for total war.

Yet it was also clear that the coalition had given a special stimulus to developing a degree of expertise in government which seemed likely to remain permanent. Ministers and officials spoke glowingly of the value of applied science and operational research. The Civil Service was compelled to reconsider the organization, pay, and conditions of all the principal professionals employed in the public sector, particularly the research scientists in government labora-tories. The techniques devised for the aggregation of economic data seemed indispensable to future governments. There was a widely acknowledged need for government economists and statis-ticians, even among those who were sceptical of the value of planning. It looked as if governments would be better equipped to make their choices. The greatest impact of short-term improvi-sation for national survival, whether or not the product of coalition, was on those fields of government activity for which outside expertise was recruited. Whitehall gained considerably from the temporary civil service which swelled the ranks of the war-time bureaucracy.

The advantages of coalition were the least obvious where they were often the most ardently pursued—in social reform and international diplomacy. In both these areas there were many fundamental problems which were not as easily transformed by mobilization as many had hoped. The doctrine of total war encouraged a great deal of speculation about the feasibility of social revolution, in spite of the very conservative assumptions behind the means of conscription and the direction of labour; the practice of joint planning with the Americans induced a lot of thinking about improving the scope of international co-operation, although it was painfully obvious that the British Empire and Commonwealth constituted a stumbling block to American ambitions in international affairs. Ministers and officials had to acknowledge their dependence on factors outside their control. In social reform and international diplomacy the coalition was not able to develop a collective view without running the risk of exposing the differences between the representatives of different political parties. The government struggled along to find a policy, but not with any evident relish or success.

The handicap of this particular coalition was the prescription of frank debate imposed by both security considerations and the intense pressure of business. Ministers and officials had become so accustomed to the many cut-off points which protected confidential information that they had almost forgotten what it meant to give voice in public to fears and hopes. The 'professionals' in politics were cocooned more tightly than usual in the apparatus of implementation. It would be ridiculous to regard their inhibitions as a conscious conspiracy of silence. But in retrospect it seems clear that their fears about what they called 'external economic relations' — Britain's future in world trade — played a part in holding the coalition together, although they provoked many deep internal divisions. Differences between ministers on how to handle discussions with the Americans could not be aired in public. Perhaps more than any other practical question, the problem of sustaining a British momentum in the continuation of the war against Japan after Germany had surrendered loomed large in the minds of ministers as the Allies' campaign in Europe progressed. The British public did not share the American commitment to the Pacific. Nor did it appear to accept the concern of the 'professionals' for the restoration of British power in the Far East. After five years of war it seemed impossible to arouse the same fervour and spirit of sacrifice to keep a British presence beside the Americans in the fight against Japan. No party could fight an election on the necessity for continued austerity; no electorate would be persuaded by the rather abstract connections which demonstrated that Britain's chances of a rapid post-war recovery in industry depended on the raw materials and markets of the Empire and Commonwealth.

Ministerial hesitations about the continued benefits of coalition in 1944-5 underlined the special circumstances which had brought the government into existence. The coalition was a product of Britain's position in European politics in the mid-1930s, not of the Allied joint planning system after 1942. It made less political sense as the conflict was extended far beyond Europe. Although American financial influence was apparent as soon as hostilities opened, there was a jump in both the quantity of resources involved and the quality of organization required between the Anglo-French co-operation of 1939-40 and the Anglo-American alliance of 1941-2. In a sense, the coalition was carried along from one form of warfare to another by the ramifications of European diplomacy, and by the fortunes of battle itself. The attack on Churchill's management of the war in 1942 was in large measure a reflection of escalation of war to world-wide proportions. If Churchill had given way to his critics in the summer of 1942, a new Prime Minister would have formed another coalition more in keeping with the times. As it happened, Churchill by sheer drive and daring kept going with the conventions he had created, and at the same time embraced the opportunity to forge the links in the Anglo-American alliance at all levels. That daring compelled a general acceptance of further effort from ministers and the public alike, even to the point when it became obvious that Churchill could no longer wield the influence he once did. The military reasons for the coalition changing its character after the winter of 1942-3 were part of the declining British contribution to the collective Allied success.

This very fundamental change in the context of the coalition's existence did not destroy the strong sense of constitutional orthodoxy which characterized its actions. Ministers and MPs saw the necessity for the executive to take supreme authority and to suspend many of the normal rules of parliamentary government; but they also wanted to ensure that the restoration of parliamentary liberties followed the normal processes of statute making. Although the coalition ministers tried to extend the methods by which the executive could control parliamentary time, they had the laudable motive of striving to accelerate the transition from war to peace by removing the anomalies of defence regulations through statutes acceptable to the House of Commons. There was never any suggestion of post-war legislation by decree. The fear that the British public would not support a final onslaught on Japan was intensified by the sheer conventionality of wishing to sustain the fight with appropriate parliamentary sanctions.

The purely American decision to drop atomic bombs on Japan removed this anxiety by bringing the war to a close fairly abruptly. Churchill without consulting the Cabinet of his caretaker administration gave a token British consent to this action at the beginning of July 1945. Two bombs were dropped—on Hiroshima on 6 August and on Nagasaki on 9 August—in the second week of the new Labour government's administration. Within three months—May, June and July—all the assumptions of central government planning were revised, and action envisaged for the transition from war to peace was accelerated on a more limited time-table.

The caution and orthodoxy of ministers and officials was a 'professional' reaction to re-establishing the basis of popular consent to government. They all recognized that the peculiar combination of acclamation for Churchill's authority and co-operation between government and voluntary agencies was a form of consent that matched the exigencies of the first two years of coalition, but not the increasing uncertainties of the next three. Nobody could identify with confidence what had happened to the traditional bases of political support in town and country, as a result of so many different activities in civil defence, rationing, and limitations on freedom of movement at the local level. The doctrine of total war had organizational consequences for the average citizen —a fully enumerated population, each person with a national identity number. The practice of civil defence led to many improvisations in linking official and voluntary effort—rescue teams, meals provision, savings drives, fostering children. The 'professionals' had some intelligence of popular reactions in their constituencies, but nothing like the reliable soundings of local government election results or agents' reports. Ministers tended to be a little suspicious of the tittle-tattle they received from constituency and party correspondents.

They also knew that the price of national survival had been dearly paid with the loss of overseas capital and a diminished international standing. The country's position could only be defended by an element of bluff in international negotiation until the industrial potential of the country could be reharnessed for exports and the payment of overseas debt. But at the same time ministers and officials could not suppress a feeling that the coalition had at least demonstrated how far the expansion of the executive branch of government had given authority to those who were prepared to convince others of their competence. The country did not lack a cadre of experienced leaders, designers, and managers. This asset seemed to provide irrefutable evidence that British parliamentary democracy had a sufficiently homogeneous social basis on which to build a more interventionist form of government. When Churchill called his coalition government 'the most capable' the country had ever had, he was only expressing a widely shared conviction that British institutions had shown themselves sufficiently adaptable to the technology of modern warfare for victory to be achieved without massive social unrest.

Notes

Introduction

1 David Butler, *Coalitions in British Politics* (1978) p. 74.
2 Maurice Cowling, *The Impact of Hitler* (1975), p. 388.
3 John Mulgan, *Report on Experience* (1947), p. 141.
4 See p. 182 below.
5 A. J. P. Taylor and others, *Churchill: four faces and the man* (1969), p. 150.
6 W. S. Churchill, *Triumph and Tragedy* (reprinted 1956), p. 225 (1st ed., p. 268).
7 J. W. Wheeler-Bennett, (ed.) *Action This Day: working with Churchill* (1968), p. 230.

Chapter 1

1 The Institute of Industrial Administration and the Institute of Personnel Management both more than doubled their memberships in the early years of the war: see John Child, *British Management Thought* (1969), p. 113.
2 B. E. V. Sabine, *British Budgets in Peace and War: 1932-1945* (1970), p. 175.
3 The Cabinet office official histories contain no history of Cabinet organizations. Norman Gibbs who was appointed to be the 'narrator' was allowed to write only for a restricted circulation. The best guide to the system is the Public Record Office Handbook No. 17 (1975) by S. S. Wilson.
4 Ewen Montagu, *Beyond Top Secret U* (1977), pp. 106-7.
5 A. W. Baldwin, *A Flying Start* (1967).
6 Clement Attlee reporting in *Labour Candidate,* No. 46 (Winter 1939). Herbert Morrison was not then in favour of Labour entering a coalition, because it lacked a sufficient number of competent ministers; see J. A. Cross, *Sir Samuel Hoare* (1977), pp. 310-11.
7 David Butler and A. H. Halsey, (eds.) *Policy and Politics* (1978), pp. 170-73.

Chapter 2

1 Ian McLaine, *Ministry of Morale* (1979), p. 31.
2 W. S. Churchill, *The Hinge of Fate* (reprint ed., 1953), p. 310.
3 Jean Monnet, *Mémoires* (English ed., 1978), p. 158.
4 The government contained only two women, both in parliamentary private secretary posts: Ellen Wilkinson (Labour) and Florence Horsburgh (Conservative).
5 Elizabeth Barker, *Churchill and Eden at War* (1978), p. 91.
6 Donald McLachan, *In the Chair* (1971), p. 201.
7 P. H. J. H. Gosden, *Education in the Second World War* (1976), p. 270.
8 Kingsley Martin, *Harold Laski* (1953), p. 151.

Chapter 3

1 Sir Ronald Wingate, *Lord Ismay* (1970), pp. 43-4.
2 J. C. Masterman, *The Double-Cross System* (1972), pp. 58-9.
3 Ronald Lewin, *Ultra Goes to War* (1978), pp. 190-91.
4 Wingate, op. cit., p. 61.
5 Solly Zuckerman, *From Apes to War Lords* (1978), p. 404.
6 P. M. S. Blackett, *Studies of War* (1962), p. 206.
7 Zuckerman, op. cit., esp. pp. 149-96.
8 Wingate, op. cit., p. 34.
9 Margaret Gowing, *Britain and Atomic Energy* (1964), p. 94.
10 Ronald Lewin, *Churchill as Warlord* (1973), pp. 136-7.
11 R. W. Thompson, *Churchill and Morton* (1976), pp. 184-5, 188.
12 John Colville, *Footprints in Time* (1976), p. 93.
13 R. V. Jones, *Most Secret War* (1978), p. 182.
14 Ronald Lewin, *Ultra Goes to War* (1978), p. 198.
15 ibid., p. 149.
16 ibid., p. 186.
17 ibid., pp. 158-9.
18 Stuart Macrae, *Winston Churchill's Toy Shop* (1971).
19 Jones, op. cit., pp. 332-3.
20 ibid., p. 83.
21 See also p. 105, below.
22 *Proceedings of the Royal Society,* Vol. 342 (1975), p. 492.
23 Gowing, op. cit., pp. 241-2.
24 Jones, op. cit., p. 531.
25 Ian McLaine, *Ministry of Morale* (1979), p. 97.
26 ibid., p. 257.
27 Colville, op. cit., p. 126.

28 John Keegan, *The Face of Battle* (1976), pp. 328-9.
29 McLaine, op. cit., p. 260.

Chapter 4

1 Some authorities include a fourth—the Ministry of Works and Buildings.
2 Lionel Robbins, *Autobiography of an Economist* (1971), p. 184.
3 Paul Addison, *The Road to 1945* (1975), p. 280.
4 House of Commons Debates, Vol. 368, col. 81.
5 See also pp. 108-10, below.
6 See Cripps's Memorandum of 30 July 1942 in CAB 127/67.
7 See also pp. 100-1, below.
8 Two agencies which were attached secretly to existing departments entailed very heavy ministerial duties—the Special Operations Executive to the Ministry of Economic Warfare and the Secret Intelligence Service to the Foreign Office. Lord Selborne, who was Minister of Economic Warfare from February 1942 onwards, said that he spent four-fifths of his time on special operations work.
9 Alan Bullock, *The Life and Times of Ernest Bevin,* Vol. 2 (1967), p. 170.
10 *People in Production* By Mass Observation for the Advertising Service Guild (ed.) (Penguin Special, 1942).
11 C. H. Stuart (ed.) *The Reith Diaries* (1975), pp. 273-87.
12 Lionel Robbins, *Autobiography of an Economist* (1971), pp. 178-9.
13 Lionel Robbins, *The Economic Problem in Peace and War* (1947), pp. 2, 68.
14 C. B. A. Behrens, *Merchant Shipping and the Demands of War* (1955), pp. 368-9.
15 Sir Norman Kipping, *Summing Up* (1972), p. 7.
16 Bullock, op. cit., Vol. 2 (1967), p. 273.
17 London School of Economics Archives, Dalton's diary: entries for 8 Feb. and 26 June 1943.
18 M. M. Postan, *British War Production* (1952), pp. 284-5.
19 See also pp. 144, 149-51, below.

Chapter 5

1 WP (44) 123 in CAB 66/47 for the Cabinet Committee report (18 Feb. 1944).
2 P. H. J. H. Gosden, *Education in the Second World War* (1976), p. 309.

3 See also pp. 149-51, below.

4 Paul Addison, *The Road to 1945* (1975), p. 188.

5 Angus Calder, *The People's War* (1971), pp. 632-4.

6 José Harris, *William Beveridge* (1977), p. 376.

7 Nuffield College Library Archives.

8 Donald McLachan, *In the Chair* (1971), p. 214.

9 W. S. Churchill, *Triumph and Tragedy* (Reprint ed., 1956), pp. 467-8.

10 Attlee papers, Bodleian Library, Oxford: Box 8.

11 ibid., 1941: 17 Feb., 22 May, 15 July; 1942: 7 Jan., 7 Oct.

12 David Howell, *British Social Democracy* (1976), p. 125.

13 Deryck Abel, *Ernest Benn: Counsel for Liberty* (1960), esp. pp. 110-12, 141, 121.

14 Public Record Office, Prem 4/87/10.

15 ibid., CAB 21/1586.

16 ibid., CAB 127/78: Cole to Cripps, 3 Nov. 1942.

17 ibid., CAB 117/43: Greenwood to Westwood, 27 Oct. 1941.

18 ibid., CAB 117/27: Baster to Hurst, 15 Jan. 1943—i.e. the Royal Institute of International Affairs, Nuffield College, Oxford, and Political and Economic Planning.

19 ibid., LAB 25/148.

20 John Colville, *Footprints in Time* (1976), p. 206.

21 Addison, op. cit., p. 237.

22 Public Record Office, T 161/1198: Minute 9 Apr. 1945.

23 ibid., Prem 4/87/12.

Chapter 6

1 Christopher Thorne, *Allies of a Kind* (1978), p. 135, on the March 1942 agreement.

2 Elizabeth Barker, *Churchill and Eden at War* (1978), p. 109.

3 W. S. Churchill, *The Hinge of Fate* (reprint ed., 1951), pp. 185-8.

4 J. P. Davies, *Dragon by the Tail* (1972), p. 274.

Conclusion

1 Brian Bond, *Liddell Hart: a study of his military thought* (1977), esp. Ch. 5.

2 Samuel Hynes, *The Auden Generation* (1976), p. 382.

3 Goronwy Rees, *A Chapter of Accidents* (1972), p. 155.

4 W. S. Churchill, *Secret Session Speeches* (1946), p. 75.

5 House of Commons Debates, Vol. 417, col. 1408.

6 Paul Hasluck, *The Government and the People,* Vol. 1 (Canberra, 1952), pp. 501-2, 505.
7 J. L. Granatstein, *Canada's War* (1975), p. 105.
8 ibid., p. 205.
9 Bond, op. cit., p. 147.
10 Lord Salisbury, *Post-War Conservative Policy* (1942).

Suggestions for further reading

My advice to anyone who wishes to take further the subject of Churchill's war-time administration is:

(**a**) get to know the standard bibliographies
e.g. (1) Margaret Gowing and A. H. K. Slater, 'Britain in the Second World War', Chapter 22 in R. Higham (ed.), *A Guide to the Sources of British Military History* (London, 1972);
(2) A. G. S. Enser, *A subject bibliography of the Second World War* (London, 1977);
(3) Gwyn M. Bayliss, *A bibliographic guide to the Two World Wars* (New York, 1978);

(**b**) do not become bogged down too soon in the many biographies and autobiographies of the principal participants (for a selection, see below);

(**c**) get a feel for the shape of the war, and then begin to explore the books which are based on the documents made available when 'the cream' of the public records from 1939 to 1945 was placed on open access in 1972 in the Public Record Office, all at the same time, instead of being released at yearly intervals. (For some indication of these works, see below.)

Books on the War

Peter Calvocoressi and Guy Wint, *Total War* (Penguin Press, 1972) is an extremely valuable introduction.

I have assumed that my readers have access to one or more of the following: Paul Addison, *The Road to 1945: British Politics and the Second World War* (1975, Quartet Books, 1977); Angus Calder, *The People's War: Britain 1939-1945* (1969, Panther Books, 1971); Basil Liddell Hart, *History of the Second World War* (1970, Pan Books, 1973); William Harrington and Peter Young, *The 1945 Revolution* (1978); Henry Pelling, *Britain and the Second World War* (1970); Gordon Wright, *The Ordeal of Total War* (1968).

Both Calder and Pelling give a useful bibliography for anyone interested in the political side of the war effort.

Churchill's own account of the war in six volumes should not be neglected. It has the directness of his own perspective, and many extracts from his own minutes and letters. I used the reprint society edition.

1 *The Gathering Storm* (1948, reprint 1950)
2 *Their Finest Hour* (1949, reprint 1951)
3 *The Grand Alliance* (1950, reprint 1952)
4 *The Hinge of Fate* (1951, reprint 1953)
5 *Closing the Ring* (1952, reprint 1954)
6 *Triumph and Tragedy* (1954, reprint 1956)

For Churchill himself, it might be interesting to look at A. J. P. Taylor and others, *Churchill: The Four Faces and the Man* (London, 1969) before reading one of the biographies. That book contains Anthony Storr's essay on Churchill's psychological make-up.

There are many books on individual battles and campaigns. Begin with an old one (e.g. Chester Wilmot, *The Struggle for Europe* (1952)) and then branch out according to the guidance given in the books above.

Do not forget the evidence of photographs and films. These have been skilfully exploited by the Open University courses and the Time-Life series. They also illustrate 'the home front', e.g.:

Tom Harrisson, *Living through the Blitz* 1976)
Arthur Marwick, *Home Front: the British and the Second World War* (1976)

The 'official histories' published by HMSO for the Cabinet Office historical section are a major set of sources used by all writers in this field, but they are 'heavy going'. Every beginner should at least

know about the six volumes devoted to *Grand Strategy* and about
W. K. Hancock and Margaret Gowing, *The British War Economy*
(1949).

Books on the Coalition

Apart from the biographies and diaries listed below, the following
suggestions are drawn from recent publications and arranged
according to the chapter headings of this book. Maxwell P.
Schoenfeld, *The War Ministry of Winston Churchill* (Iowa State
University Press, 1972), was based on material published before
1969, and before the influence of the opening of the public records
was fully felt.

General (Chapters 1 and 2)
T. D. Burridge, *British Labour and Hitler's War* (1976)
D. Butler (ed.), *Coalitions in British Politics* (1978)
Ian McLaine, *Ministry of Morale* (1979)

Strategy (Chapter 3)
Ronald Lewin, *Churchill as Warlord* (1973) *Ultra Goes to War* (1978)
J. C. Masterman, *The Double Cross System* (Yale and London,
1972)
Stephen Roskill, *Churchill and the Admirals* (1977)
F. W. Winterbotham, *Ultra Secret* (1974)

Economy (Chapter 4)
Alan S. Milward, *War, Economy, and Society, 1939-1945* (1977)
J. M. Keynes, Collected Writings (ed. D. Moggridge), Vol. XXII,
Activities 1939-1945: Internal War Finance (1978)

Social Reform (Chapter 5)
José Harris, *William Beveridge* (1977)
P. H. J. H. Gosden, *Education in the Second World War* (1976)

Diplomacy (Chapter 6)
Elizabeth Barker, *Churchill and Eden at War* (1978)
W. Roger Louis, *Imperialism at bay: the United States and the
decolonisation of the British Empire, 1941-45* (1978)
Christopher Thorne, *Allies of a Kind: the United States, Britain
and the War against Japan, 1941-45* (1978)

Biographies

Biographies—the name of the politician is followed, where applicable, by the title of his autobiography covering 1939-45, then the name of his principal biographer.

(a) Ministers in the War Cabinet

Anderson, Wheeler-Bennett (1962); **Attlee**, *As It Happened* (1954) **Beaverbrook**, A. J. P. Taylor (1972); **Bevin**, Alan Bullock (1960, 1967); **Casey**, *Personal Experience* (1962); **Chamberlain**, Keith Feiling (1946), Dilks and Beattie (forthcoming); **Churchill**, *Second World War* (6 Vols., 1948-54) (see above), Henry Pelling (1974), Martin Gilbert (forthcoming); **Cripps**, C. A. Cooke (1957), Maurice Shock (forthcoming); **Eden**, *Facing the Dictators* (1962); **Greenwood**, G. McDermott (forthcoming); **Halifax**, *Fullness of Days* (1957), Birkenhead (1965); **Woolton**, *Memoirs* (1959).

(b) other Ministers

Amery, *My Political Life* (3 Vols., 1953-5) (forthcoming); **H. Balfour**, *Wings over Westminster* (1973); **Bracken**, Andrew Boyle (1974), C. E. Lysaght (1979); **R. A. Butler**, *Art of the Possible* (1971), Roy Harrod (1959); **Cherwell**, Birkenhead (1961); **Duff Cooper**, *Old Men Forget* (1953); **Dalton**, *Fateful Years* (1957); **P. J. Grigg**, *Prejudice and Judgement* (1948); **Hankey**, Stephen Roskill Vol. 3 (1974); **Harold Macmillan**, *The Blast of War* (1967), A. Sampson (1967); **Simon**, *Retrospect* (1952); **Swinton**, *I Remember* (1948), J. A. Cross (forthcoming).

(c) temporary civil servants

Beveridge, *Power and Influence* (1953), Jose Harris (1978); **Colville**, *Footprints in Time* (1976); **R. V. Jones**, *My Secret War* (1978); **N. Kipping**, *Summing Up* (1972); **M. Muggeridge**, *Chronicles of Wasted Time* Vol. 2 (1973); **L. Robbins**, *Autobiography of an Economist* (1971); **Wheeler-Bennett** (ed.) *Action this Day* (1969), *Special Relationships* (1975).

Diaries

Chips Channon (ed. R. Rhodes James) (1967); Sir Alexander Cadogan (ed. David Dilks) (1971); Cecil King, *With Malice Toward None* (1970); Harold Nicolson (ed. Nigel Nicolson), Vol. 2 (1967); Lord Reith (ed. C. H. Stuart) (1975); Evelyn Waugh (ed. Michael Davie) (1976); (N.B. Dalton's diary is unpublished: L. S. E. Archives).

Index

DATE DUE

GAYLORD   PRINTED IN U.S.A.